Asset Prices, Booms and Recessions

Springer

Berlin
Heidelberg
New York
Hong Kong
London
Milan
Paris
Tokyo

Willi Semmler

Asset Prices, Booms and Recessions

Financial Market, Economic Activity and the Macroeconomy

With 33 Figures
and 22 Tables

 Springer

Willi Semmler

Center for Empirical Macroeconomics
Bielefeld University
Universitätsstraße 25
33615 Bielefeld, Germany
e-mail: wsemmler@wiwi.uni-bielefeld.de
and
Department of Economics
Graduate Faculty
New School University
65 Fifth Ave,
New York, NY 10003, USA
e-mail: semmlerw@newschool.edu

ISBN 3-540-00432-7 Springer-Verlag Berlin Heidelberg New York

Cataloging-in-Publication Data applied for
A catalog record for this book is available from the Library of Congress.

Bibliographic information published by Die Deutsche Bibliothek
Die Deutsche Bibliothek lists this publication in the Deutsche Nationalbibliografie;
detailed bibliographic data available in the internet at *http.//dnb.ddb.de*

Springer-Verlag Berlin Heidelberg New York
a member of BertelsmannSpringer Science + Business Media GmbH

http://www.springer.de
© Springer-Verlag Berlin Heidelberg 2003
Printed in Germany

The use of general descriptive names, registered names, trademarks, etc. in this publication does not imply, even in the absence of a specific statement, that such names are exempt from the relevant protective laws and regulations and therefore free for general use.

Cover design: Erich Kirchner, Heidelberg

SPIN 10911266   42/3130 – 5 4 3 2 1 0 – Printed on acid-free paper

Preface

This book is on the economics of asset prices, booms and recessions. More particularly we study the interaction of the financial market and economic activity from a macroeconomic perspective. The book is introductory in the sense that it sets out a dynamic framework to study the financial-real interaction. The financial market to be considered here encompasses the money and bond market, credit market, stock market and foreign exchange market. Economic activity is described by the activity of firms, banks, households, governments and countries. We study how the performance of the financial market, financial market volatility and instability affect economic activity and we show how economic activity feeds back to asset prices and the performance of the financial market.

The focus in this book is on theories, dynamic models and empirical evidence of the interrelation of the financial market, economic activity and the macroeconomy. Applications can be found to the interaction of financial market, economic activity and the macroeconomy of the US, Latin American, Asian as well as Euro-area countries. We also consider cases and episodes of financial instability and financial crises and their impact on economic activity and how this can be explained by economic theory.

Although linear and nonlinear econometric methods are used here a more extensive treatment of those econometric methods to estimate dynamic relationships in economics and finance is given in Wöhrmann and Semmler (2002). The manuscript can be found at www.wiwi.uni-bielefeld.de/~semmler/cem.

The book is based on lectures given at the University of Bielefeld and New School University, New York. I want to thank colleagues as well as several generations of students who took the class on the "Financial Market, Economic Activity and the Macroeconomy". Many chapters of this book have also been presented at conferences, workshops and seminars in the US, France, Belgium, Austria, Italy, Spain and Germany. I, in particular, want to thank Gaby Windhorst for typing many versions of the manuscript, Jens Rubart, Lucas Bernard, and Leanne Ussher for their assistance in editing this book in LaTeX and Uwe Koeller and Mark Meyer for preparing the figures. I also want to thank Sabine Guschwa for providing the data set for the estimation in Chap. 4.4 and Peter Wöhrmann for many years of fruitful discussions and collaboration. Finally I want to thank my various co-authors who have allowed me to draw on our joint work. In particular, I want to thank Toichiro Asada, Reiner Franke, Carl Chiarella, Chih-ying Hsiao, Peter Flaschel, Gang Gong, Martin Lettau, Levent Kockesen, Malte Sieveking and Peter Wöhrmann.

Contents

Those who want to be rich in a day, will be hanged in a year.
(Leonardo da Vinci, 1452–1519)

Introduction

Financial markets perform the essential role of channelling funds to firms that have productive investment opportunities. Financial markets also permit households and governments to borrow against future income. Countries borrow from abroad in order to speed up growth. The growth of financial markets has exerted its impact on economic growth, employment and economic policies. Financial markets have grown due to financial deepening and financial liberalization. Financial deepening is a result of financial innovations and recently developed financial instruments such as financial derivatives. Moreover, financial liberalization has actively been advocated by the IMF and the World Bank and has been pursued by many governments since the 1980s. Yet, during the last 20 years almost all countries have experienced major episodes of financial instability sometimes with devastating effects. The Mexican (1994), the Asian (1997–1998) and the Russian (1998) financial crises constitute three examples wherein a fast liberalization of financial markets has led to a currency crisis, sudden reversal of capital flows followed by financial instability and consequent decline in economic activity.[1] Also recently, after a long time period of asset price over-valuation, in the years 2001–2002 another important episode of asset price depreciation and financial market instability occurred in advanced industrial countries, in the US and in the countries of the Euro-area. Here after the long IT-stock market bubble doubtful practices of financial engineering and balance sheet fraud by numerous large firms have been discovered. This led to a general distrust of the public in the equity market with consequently high volatility and then a strong downward trend in equity prices. On the other hand, the globalization and the volatility of the financial markets have also been seen as a new opportunity for financial market traders and investment firms.

Our book deals with the financial market and its relationship to economic activity. At the outset, let us, however, first state what we mean by the financial market and economic activity. A basic part of the financial market is the money and bond market. This is where, to a great extent, short and long-term interest rates are determined. A second important part is the credit market where either commercial papers are traded or where households and firms obtain bank loans. In fact, as we will see, bank credit is still the most dominant source of finance for real activity (firms, households). Yet, credit may also depend on asset prices. Thus credit, credit risk and asset prices will be important for our considerations. A third important financial market is the

---

[1] For details, see Stiglitz (2002).

stock market. Most asset or security pricing theories refer to the equity market. A fourth type of financial market pertains to the international capital market where lending and borrowing across national borders and foreign exchange markets come into play. Economic activity is described by the activity of firms, households, banks, governments and countries.

The book will pursue the following questions.

- What are the specifics of the major financial markets and do they differ in importance for economic activity? Does the deepening and liberalization of the financial market stimulate or retard economic growth? Will developed financial markets lead to a more efficient use of resources?
- Has the deepening of the financial markets and liberalization decreased or increased the volatility of macroeconomic variables such as output, employment, trade accounts, long term interest rates, exchange rates, money wages, the price level and stock prices? Has financial risk increased and will financial liberalization lead to booms and crashes?
- What theories explain the relationship between economic activity, asset prices and returns? What economic, in particular macroeconomic, factors are important for asset prices and returns? How do asset prices and returns behave over the business cycle. Do the equity premium and Sharpe-ratio, a measure of the risk-return trade-off, move with the business cycle?
- Are asset price inflation and deflation and financial market volatility harmful for economic activity? How do asset prices, by themselves or through the credit channel, impact the business cycle? How strong is the financial accelerator in contrast to the real accelerator? How can financial market instability be explained and how useful are models of multiple equilibria to explain financial crises and large output losses of countries?
- Do monetary and fiscal policies impact the financial market and how do financial markets impact government policies? How effective are these policies in open economies with free capital flows and volatile exchange rates? Can and how should financial markets be regulated? Should governments or monetary authorities intervene to stabilize asset prices?

These are some of the major questions we want to pursue in subsequent chapters.

Theoretical and empirical work on the relationship of financial and real activities have been undertaken by different economic schools. One currently highly visible school refers to the theory of perfect capital markets. Perfect capital markets are mostly assumed in intertemporal general equilibrium theory (stochastic growth and Real Business Cycle (RBC) theory). Yet, there is no interaction of credit, asset prices and real activity. In contrast to this many theoretical and empirical studies have applied the theory of imperfect capital markets. Moreover, there are other traditions like the Keynesian tradition (revived, for example, by Tobin 1980 and Minksy 1975) that have been very influential on macro modelling and macroeconometric approaches to study the interaction between the financial market and economic activity. There is currently also another important view on this interaction. This is represented by

Shiller's (1991, 2001) overreaction hypothesis. The research that will be presented here is influenced strongly by Keynesian tradition, yet we also draw upon recent development in information economics, as developed by Stiglitz and others, who have attempted to systematically describe how actual financial markets operate.

Many studies on the financial market claim that a crucial impediment to the functioning of the financial system is asymmetric information, a situation in which one agent of a financial contract has much less information than the other. Borrowers, for example, who take out loans, usually have much better information about potential returns of investment projects and risk associated with the projects than lenders. Asymmetric information leads to two other basic problems: adverse selection and moral hazard.[2]

Asymmetric information leads to adverse selection since the worst borrowers, i.e. borrowers with the potential of bad credit risks are the ones who most actively seek out loans; they may offer a high interest rate, since they are likely not to repay the loan. Thus the parties that most likely produce an undesirable (adverse) outcome are most likely to be selected. Since adverse selection may lead to heavy loan losses for lenders, lenders may decide not to make any loan even though there are good borrowers in the market.

Moral hazard occurs after the transaction has taken place. Lenders are subject to hazards since the borrower has incentives to engage in activities that are undesirable (immoral) from the lenders point of view. Moral hazard occurs when the borrower does well when the project succeeds but the lender bears most of the cost when the project fails. Borrowers may also use loans inefficiently, for example they may use loans for personal expenditure. Lenders may impose restrictions, face screening and enforcement costs and this may lead to credit rationing even for potentially good borrowers.

The existence of asymmetric information, adverse selection and moral hazard also explains why there is an important role for the government to play in the regulation and supervision of the financial market. Regulation and supervision has the task of enhancing information and minimizing adverse selection and moral hazard problems. This requires the production of information through screening and monitoring. Firms and banks need to be required to adhere to standards of accounting and publicly reveal information about their sales, assets and earnings. Fast liberalization of the financial market is therefore not without risk if there is insufficient financial market regulation, inexperienced and loose supervision, no disclosure requirement, limited screening and monitoring of financial institutions and no secure safety net for the financial institutions (for example, insurance for bank deposits) as well as for the population in general.

Those above three concepts, asymmetric information, adverse selection and moral hazard have been employed, for example, by Mishkin (1998) and others to explain the Asian financial crisis of the years 1997–1998. A theory along similar lines, also referring to firms' and banks' deteriorating balance sheets, can be found in Krugman (1999a,b). Miller and Stiglitz (1999) employ a multiple equilibria model to explain

---

[2]For a more detailed explanation of those terms, see Stiglitz (2002) and Mishkin (1998)

financial crisis. Whereas those theories point to the perils of too fast a liberalization of financial markets and point to the role of government bank supervision and guarantees. Burnside, Eichenbaum and Rebelo (1999) view government guarantees as cause for financial crisis. These authors argue that the lack of private hedging of exchange rate risk by firms and banks led to the financial crisis in Asia. Other authors, following the bank run model by Diamond and Dybvig (1983) (see for example, Chang and Velasco (1999)) argue that financial crises occur if there is a lack of short run liquidity. Further surveys of financial crisis models and discussion of policy issues can be found in Edwards (1999) and Rogoff (1999) who discuss the role of the IMF as the lender of last resort.

As above shown, many observes of the financial crisis in emerging markets in the years 1997–1999 were very quick to blame loose standards of accounting, the lack of safety nets such as insurance for bank deposits and the lack of supervision of banks and financial institutions as having caused the financial crisis in emerging markets. Yet the years 2001 and 2002 have shown that even advanced industrial regions such as the US, the Euro-area and Yen-area have not escaped excessive asset price volatility and financial instability. As has turned out the same loose accounting practices by corporations and by auditing firms, the lack of supervision by the executive boards of firms and regulatory institutions and the role of big banks helping to disguise huge corporate debt has led to a general distrust by shareholders and the general public in fair asset pricing by the market. The consequence was a financial episode with large asset price depreciation in the US and Euro-area in the years 2001–2002.

The content of the book is as follows. Part I deals with money, bonds and economic activity. In Chap. 1 we consider the basis of the money and bond markets and the role of monetary policy determining interest rates. Chapter 2 elaborates on interest rates which play an important role for economic activity as well as for asset and derivative pricing. We will study the determination of short and long-term interest rates and the term structure of interest rates both from the point of view of theory as well as empirical evidence.

Part II, treats the credit market and economic activity. In Chap. 3 and 4, we will present theories and empirical evidence on the credit market, i.e. borrowing and lending, and the causes and consequences of credit risk. We focus on the theory of perfect and imperfect capital markets and the role of the banking system for the relationship of credit and economic activity by positing that firms and households finance their activity largely through credit market instruments such as bank loans or commercial papers. We also show that asset prices play an important role for the credit market.

A further important part of the financial market is the stock market. Part III deals with the stock market and economic activity. In Chaps. 5, 6 and 7 we study the equity market as a large part of the security market and explore the approaches that focus on the interaction of asset pricing and economic activity.

In Part IV, Chaps. 8–10, we will elaborate on asset pricing theories such as the Capital Asset Pricing Model (CAPM), the Present Value (PV) approach and the consumption and production based intertemporal asset pricing theory. An important issue in Part III as well as Part IV will be the relation of stock market volatility, credit excess asset returns, credit and economic activity and to what extent stylized facts can be explained by macroeconomic models, intertemporal asset pricing models (consumption based and production based asset pricing theories), stochastic growth models and some non-conventional approaches such as Shiller's overreaction theory or heterogenous agent models.

Part V focuses on the foreign exchange market, financial instability and economic activity. In Chap. 11, by using macroeconomic portfolio approach, we first present an integrated view of the money, credit, bond and equity markets in a unified framework. We will here refer to the portfolio approach developed by Tobin and study the relation of the financial sector, as it appears in the portfolio theory, to economic activity. The main tool used here are the balance sheets of economic agents to discuss the financial sector. This helps us to explain financial instabilities, financial crises and declining economic activity entailing large output losses that occasionally occur in certain countries or regions. Whereas in Chap. 11 the role of balance sheets for financial instability is explored, in Chap. 12 an attempt will be undertaken to include also the foreign exchange market and international borrowing and lending in our study of the financial market and economic activity. Here we focus on the volatility of exchange rates, credit market, asset prices and the spill-over effects to real activity.

Finally, Chap. 13 draws some policy conclusions. Useful econometric toolkits for studying linear and nonlinear dynamic relationships in economics and finance are summarized in Wöhrmann and Semmler (2002).

Part I

Money, Bonds and Economic Activity

Chapter 1
Money, Bonds and Interest Rates

1.1 Introduction

We start this book on the financial market and economic activity with money, bonds and interest rates. Interest rates are major determining factors for asset markets. Interest rate processes are important for credit markets, equity markets, commercial paper markets, foreign exchange markets and security pricing such as stocks, bonds and options. Interest rates are important for real activity, consumption and investment spending. Interest rate spreads and the term structure of interest rates affect asset markets as well as real activity. In this chapter we study some major issues in the theory and empirics of interest rates. We will give here only some elementary expositions. [1]

We will first define what money is and how monetary theories help us to determine the interest rate. We will refer to the loanable fund theory and the Keynesian liquidity preference theory. If there are only two assets, money and bonds, either of them can be used to explain interest rates. We will define the different types of bonds and different types of monetary policy aimed at stabilizing inflation and output. In the next chapter we discuss short- and long-term interest rates and the term structure of interest rates.

1.2 Some Basics

In modern monetary economies money serves as the medium of exchange, unit of account and store of value. On the international level it also can serve as the medium of international reserve. In the latter case usually only a few currencies have been selected, for example the US Dollar, the Euro or the Yen. Historically, money has developed from metallic money (gold or silver) to fiat money (paper currency) backed by the monetary authority of the country. Monetary aggregates are usually referred to as M_1, M_2 and M_3 money. The subsequent scheme defines those aggregates:

---

[1] A more detailed treatment of bonds and interest rates can be found in Mishkin, 1995 (Chaps. 1–7).

Monetary aggregates:

$$M_1 = \text{currency} \quad + \quad \left\{ \begin{array}{l} \text{traveller checks} \\ \text{demand deposit} \\ \text{other checkable deposits} \end{array} \right.$$

$$M_2 = M_1 \quad + \quad \left\{ \begin{array}{l} \text{time deposits} \\ \text{saving deposits} \end{array} \right.$$

$$M_3 = M_2 \quad + \quad \left\{ \begin{array}{l} \text{large time deposits} \\ \text{money market mutual funds} \end{array} \right.$$

$$L = M_3 \quad + \quad \left\{ \begin{array}{l} \text{short-term Treasury securities} \\ \text{commercial papers} \end{array} \right.$$

Hereby L represents liquidity. Monetary policy when aiming at controlling monetary aggregates usually selects one of these aggregates to stabilize inflation or output.

1.3 Macroeconomic Theories of the Interest Rate

Traditionally, in monetary economics, there have been two basic theories of interest rate determination. These are the loanable fund theory and the liquidity preference theory. The first theory originates in classical monetary theory of David Hume and David Ricardo. The second is based on Keynes' work. Both give us a theory of interest rate determination. We give a brief introduction to both theories.[2]

1. Loanable Funds Theory

Before we define the theory of loanable fund we want to define some simple principles of bond pricing. Bonds are simple loans that are traded on the bond market. They comprise principle and interest payments. A coupon bond is a bond with a face value F, of say 1000 that pays a fixed amount of income, say 100, so the interest rate is $i = \frac{100}{1000}$. A discount bond (zero coupon bond) can be obtained at a price below the face value so that the interest rate is $i = \frac{1000-900}{900}$. The value of a console (permanent coupon payment) is given by the present value of the income stream from the bond, $\frac{100}{0.1} = 1000$. A current yield is $i_c = \frac{C}{P_b}$ with C the annual payment and P_b the price of the bond. A return on a bond is defined as $R_{t+1} = \frac{(C + P_{t+1} - P_t)}{P_t}$ whereby P_t is the price of the bond at period t. For our Fig. 1.1 assume

$$i = \frac{F - P_d}{P_d}$$

whereby P_d is the purchase price of the bond and F the face value of the bond.

---

[2]For more details of the subsequent basic description of the money and bond markets, see Mishkin 1995, Chaps. 2–7)

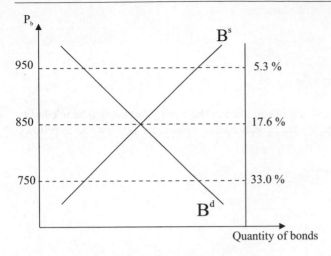

Fig. 1.1. Demand and supply of bonds

The above figure shows the demand and supply of bonds. The purchase price of the bond is on the left axis and the corresponding interest rate on the right axis. So the purchase price of the bond is inversely related to the interest rate. The interest rate – or the price of the bond – at which demand and supply of bonds are equal define equilibrium interest rates or bond prices. On the other hand, there are long-run influences on the demand and supply of bonds which are not shown in the figure. Forces that shift the demand for bonds are defined next (whereby the arrow indicates in what direction the demand is shifting)

$$
\text{Shift in the demand for bonds:} \begin{cases}
1. \text{ wealth } (B^d \rightarrow) \\
2. \text{ expected interest rate rise } (B^d \leftarrow) \\
3. \text{ inflation rate } (B^d \leftarrow) \\
4. \text{ risk } (B^d \leftarrow) \\
5. \text{ liquidity } (B^d \rightarrow)
\end{cases}
$$

The main force to affect the shift of the supply of bonds are government deficits. These can be written as $\dot{B} = iB + G - T$ whereby G is government expenditure, T government taxes (revenues) and $\dot{B}$ the change of government bonds. Assuming that government expenditures are not financed by money creation the deficit is then solely increasing the supply of government bonds.

2. Liquidity Preference Theory

The liquidity preference theory originates in Keynes (1936) and can, in a simplified version, be considered the logical counterpart of the loanable fund theory if we assume an asset market with two assets only. So we might suppose that there is supply and demand of money and bonds

$$B^s + M^s = B^d + M^d$$

So we get

$$B^s - B^d = M^d - M^s$$

Whenever the bond market is in equilibrium the money market will be in equilibrium, too. The liquidity theory can be shown to determine the interest rate as follows.

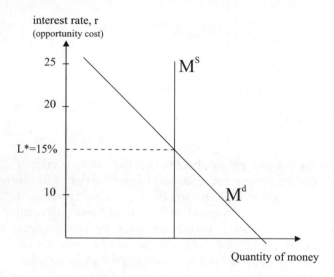

Fig. 1.2. Liquidity preference theory

Here again we might think about the forces that shift the demand for money. These are:

$$\text{Shift in the demand for money:} \begin{cases} 1. \text{ income } (M^d \rightarrow) \\ 2. \text{ price level } (M^d \rightarrow) \end{cases}$$

Shift in supply of money is solely at the discretion of the monetary authority. Making use of the standard LM-equation of the macroeconomic textbook we can write:

$$M^s = PYe^{-\alpha_1 i}$$

where Y is income and P the price level.

Taking logs with $m = \log M$, $p = \log P$, we get

$$m - p = y - \alpha_1 i$$

It follows that

$$i = \frac{y - (m - p)}{\alpha_1}$$

or

$$i = \delta y - \delta(m - p); \delta = 1/\alpha_1$$

Thus, any change in the money supply will shift the money supply curve to the right in the LM schedule and decrease the interest rate. More specifically we want to discuss two important policies that affect the interest rate.

1.4 Monetary Policy and Interest Rates

In fact there are two monetary policy rules that have recently been discussed. The first policy rule, originating in the monetarist view of the working of a monetary economy, can be formulated as follows.

(1) Control of the monetary aggregates:
This view prevailed during a short period in the 1980s in the US and, until recently at the German Bundesbank. It can formally be written by using the following equations.

$$MV = PY$$

Then, with V a constant, and taking logs we can write for growth rates,

$$\hat{m} = \hat{p} + \hat{y}$$

From this we get the p*-concept:

$$\hat{m} = \hat{p}^* + \hat{y}^*$$

with $\hat{m}$ = constant.

Hereby, the growth rate of money supply, $\hat{m}$, has to be set such that it equals $\hat{p}^*$, the target rate of inflation, plus $\hat{y}^*$, the potential output growth. As can be noted, the above inflation rate, although there is a target for it, is only indirectly targeted through the growth rate of money supply. A further disadvantage is that given an unstable money demand function – which is usually found in the data – this concept is not a very robust one, i.e., shifts in the money demand will create problems for the monetary authority in stabilizing the inflation rate.

(2) Control of the short-term interest rates:
To describe this type of monetary policy the following equation can be used.

$$r_{t+1} = r_0 + \beta_r(r_t - r_0) + \beta_p(\hat{p}_t - \pi_t) + \beta_u(y - y^*)$$
$$\text{(interest gap)} \qquad \text{(inflation gap)} \quad \text{(output gap)}$$

Here, π_t is the inflation rate targeted by the central bank, r_t the short-term interest rate, y actual and y^* the potential output. The β_i are reaction coefficients that determine how strongly the monetary authority stresses interest rate smoothing, inflation stabilization and output stabilization.

This concept originates in Taylor (1999). Svensson (1997) has demonstrated its appliction to OECD countries and it has become the dominant paradigm in central banks' monetary policy. It has the advantage that the inflation rate is directly targeted and is, therefore, called inflation targeting by the central bank. The central bank is made accountable for its targets and efforts and the decision making process is rendered more transparent. The European Central Bank (ECB) originally followed the first concept stabilizing inflation through controlling monetary aggregates. It had been argued that the German Bundesbank had achieved a solid reputation in keeping the inflation rate down with monetary targeting. However, since the second concept, of direct inflation targeting is more realistic by not relying on the (unstable) money demand function, it has been more emphasized by the ECB. The stabilizing properties of these two monetary policy rules are studied in a macroeconometric framework in Flaschel, Semmler and Gong (2001). There it is found that, by and large the first rule, since it is a direct feedback rule, has better stabilizing properties. Usually, the above interest rate reaction function, the Taylor rule, is studied for closed economies. A notable exception is the work by Ball (1999) who studies monetary policy rules for an open economy.

Note, however, that in either of the above cases the monetary authority can only directly affect the short-term interest rate. The long-term interest rates and the term structure of interest rates is affected by the financial market. In Chap. 2 we deal with the term structure of interest rates.

1.5 Monetary Policy and Asset Prices

It is the task of central banks not only to care about inflation rates and unemployment but also about the stability of the financial sector and possibly about asset prices. In most countries the central bank is also the lender of last resort.

An interesting feature of the monetary and financial environment in industrial countries over the past decade has been that inflation rates remained relatively stable and low, while the prices of equities, bonds, and foreign exchanges experienced a strong volatility with the liberalization of the financial markets. Central banks, therefore have become concerned with such volatility. The question has been raised whether such volatility is justifiable on the basis of economic fundamentals. A question that has become important is whether a monetary policy should be pursued that takes financial markets and asset price stabilization into account. In order to answer this question, it is necessary to model the relationship between asset prices and the real economy. Extended models, going beyond the one underlying the above interest rate reaction of the central bank, are needed to take into account the central bank's task to stabilize asset prices. An early study of such type can be found in Blanchard (1981) who has analyzed the relationship between stock value, output and the interest rate under different scenarios. Recent examples of models incorporating the central bank's task of stabilizing asset prices include Bernanke and Gertler (2000), Smets (1997), Kent and Lowe (1997), Dupor (2001), Cecchetti et al. (2002) and Semmler and Zhang (2002).

The difference of the approach by Semmler and Zhang (2002) from others lies in the fact that they employ a different framework. Bernanke and Gertler (2000), for example, by using a representative agent model, analyze how output and inflation will be affected by different monetary policy rules, which may or may not take into account asset price bubbles. The work by Semmler and Zhang (2002) aims at deriving optimal policy rules under the assumption that asset price bubbles do affect output and even inflation (asset prices may also affect the real economy through other channels e.g., credit channel, see Chap. 12 for example). The paper by Semmler and Zhang (2002) analyzes the effects of policy rules on output and inflation both with and without asset prices considered and show that welfare improving results are obtained if the central bank directly targets asset prices.

We note that there are, of course, other means of decreasing asset price volatility and preventing its adverse impact on the macroeconomy. As remarked above, the improvement of the stability of financial institutions and financial market supervision and regulation undertaken by the central bank appear to be the most important means toward this end. Yet, given financial institutions and financial market regulations an important contribution of the central bank might be in stabilizing output, inflation and asset prices when asset prices are volatile.

1.6 Conclusions

In this chapter we have summarized some basic theories on money, bonds and interest rates. The reader might want to also look at the actual empirical trends in monetary variables for some economies. For the US, for example, those trends can be found in Mishkin (1995, Chaps. 1–7). There, one can find trends in money supply and the price level, the correlation of the different monetary aggregates, trends in real interest rates, the business cycle and money growth rates, trends in bond rates (public and private bonds) and an example of the term structure of interest rates. Those empirical trends and stylized facts are important for a study of the financial market and the macroeconomy, since theoretical models should be able to explain such empirical trends and facts.

Chapter 2
Term Structure of Interest Rates

2.1 Introduction

We will introduce some definitions of the various terms used in the study of the term structure of interest rates and provide some economic theories that attempt to explain the term structure. After that we will summarize some empirical work on the term structure of the interest rates and show how one can model the interest rate process as a stochastic process. As we will show stochastic processes are very useful tools for interest rate and, more generally, financial market analysis. Basic stochastic processes are summarized in Appendix 1.

2.2 Definitions and Theories

We will first give some formal definitions of the terms used in the theory of the term structure of interest rates, also called yield curve.[1]

For a zero coupon bond and a full spectrum of maturities $u \in [t, T]$ and a price of the bond B(u, t) the spectrum of yields $\{R_t^u, u \in [t, T]\}$ is called term structure of interest rates, where

$$B(u,t) = 100 \, e^{-R_t^u \, (u-t)}, \; t < u \tag{2.1}$$

For example, take $R_t^u = r$ then one can compute the present value of an income stream with r the discount rate. If the income occurs at period $u > t$ and is 100 then we can write the present value of the income

$$B(u,t) = \underbrace{100}_{\text{paid at period u}} \times \underbrace{e^{-r(u-t)}}_{\text{discount factor}} \tag{2.2}$$

For example, for a given information get I_t the price of a bond that pays 100 after three periods gives us the discrete time formula

---

[1]For a more detailed technical description of the following, see Neftci (1996, Chap. 16)

$$B(3,1) = E \left[\underbrace{\frac{100}{(1+r_1)(1+r_2)(1+r_3)}}_{} \mid I_t \right] \qquad (2.3)$$

discounting by the expected short term interest rates

If we have a time varying discount factor r_s we get the following modification

$$B(u,t) = 100\, E \left[e^{-\int_t^u r_s\, ds} \mid I_t \right] \qquad (2.4)$$

If we have the price of a bond, determined by (2.4), we can calculate the yield (and the spectrum of yields)

$$R_t^u = \frac{\log B(u,t) - \log(100)}{t - u} \qquad (2.5)$$

The above relates the bond prices (the spectrum of bond prices) to the yield (spectrum of yields). Equating (2.1) and (2.4) and applying logs on both sides gives

$$R_t^u = log\, E \left[e^{-\int_t^u r_s\, ds} \mid I_t \right] \qquad (2.6)$$

Note that in continuous time the slope of the yield curve is dR_t^u/du.

Moreover, we can define forward rates (on a loan that begins at time u and matures at T) as:

$$F(t,u,T) = \frac{\log\, B(u,t) - \log\, B(T,t)}{T - u}; \; t < u < T$$

The instantaneous forward rate is:

$$f(t,u) = \lim_{T \to u} F(t,u,T); \; f(t,t) = r_t$$

The spot rate can be defined as the interest rate paid on a dollar borrowed at time s, where $t<s<T$ and held an infinitesimal period of time.

Empirically, short- and long-term interest rates usually move together and the yield curve is mostly upward sloping, but sometimes it is flat or downward sloping. In addition, there is some mean reverting process: if the short term interest rate is low one expects some high interest rates in the future and the reverse holds, if the current interest rate is high. There is some economic theory that gives us some guidance in the study of the empirical behavior of the term structure of nominal the interest rates.[2] In economic theory the yield curve is seen to be determined by

1. *expectations about the future path of r_t* :

   In the standard approach, bonds with different maturities are perfect substitutes and, given rational expectations, the expected interest rate on long term bonds is given by the expected future short term interest rates. If one thinks, for example,

---

[2]For details, see Mishkin (1995, Chap. 7)

about the short-term interest rate following some mean reverting process and the current r_t is low the expected r_t would be high. Thus, expected future interest rates would tend to rise. This theory cannot sufficiently explain why the yield curve is mostly upward sloping.

2. *segmented markets:*
Here it is assumed that bonds with different maturities are determined in different markets. Interest rates of bonds with different maturities are determined by supply and demand of bonds with those maturities. This theory can explain why the yield curve has an upward slope, but it cannot explain why interest rates of bonds with different maturities usually move together.

3. *liquidity premium:*
This theory posits that a positive term (liquidity) premium must be offered to buyers of long term bonds to compensate them for the higher risk. If one thinks of a liquidity premium as a compensation for risk then the future interest rate should include a risk premium and the term structure should always be upward sloping. Although it can explain the upward slope it needs to assume substantial fluctuations in the term premiums for long term bonds.

On the other hand, as aforementioned, it is useful for financial analysis to model the expected interest rate process – the expected short term interest rates – as a stochastic process. Take r as the short term interest rate. Then a stochastic process might be defined such as

$$dr = a(r_t, t)dt + \sigma(r_t, t)dW_t \tag{2.7}$$

where the first term on the right hand side is the drift term and the second the diffusion term with dW_t the increment of a Brownian motion. Then (2.7) can be used for (2.6). Details of such processes as (2.7) are discussed in Appendix 1. Next we will employ a specific stochastic process to model the movement of the short term interest rate.

2.3 Empirical Tests on the Term Structure

As already mentioned[3] above, a standard view on the term structure of interest rates is that the term structure can be inferred from expected future short term interest rates. Accordingly, the term structure of interest rates is given by the expected future short rates. As aforementioned, modeling and estimating expected short rates is essential for credit markets, equity and derivative markets and foreign exchange markets as well as real activity such as consumption and investment spending.

One usually attempts to capture the process of the short-term interest rate in a stochastic equation which describes the future path of the short term interest rate. The process, describing the interest rate path, is particularly useful for derivative contracts for example on stocks, bonds or foreign exchange. Often the value of the

---

[3]Details of this section can be found in Hsiao and Semmler (1999).

underlying asset is formulated in reference to a stochastic process of the short term interest rate. The Appendix 1 describes several of such stochastic processes which might be employed to model and estimate interest rate processes and the movements of other asset prices. Recently the mean reverting process has been used by a number of researchers for formulating and estimating the process of short term interest rates. For a detailed survey of recent studies, see Chan et al. (1992). This is called a one factor approach to modelling interest rates.

On the other hand, recent models have extended this approach to a two factor model. Thus, econometric regression studies on the process of short-term interest rates have also used information on longer-term rates to forecast future short-term rates. Long rates are the second factor. Examples of this approach can be found in Fama (1984), Fama and Bliss (1987), Mankiw (1996) and Campbell and Shiller (1992). Following Balduzzi (1997) we in particular assume that longer maturity bond yields incorporate useful information about the central tendency – the mean – of the short term rates. We propose a simplified version of the more complex model by Balduzzi (1997) who allows for an additional stochastic process to determine the central tendency. In our case the mean reversion process is simply determined by the spread between two long rates. We show that the spread between two longer maturity bond rates gives, for periods of stronger changes of the central tendency, additional significant information of the mean of the short rate.

Technically, in our estimations we propose the Euler approach of turning a continuous time stochastic process into a discrete time estimable process. As our experiment with a univariate stochastic process has shown the discrete time Euler estimation appears to be a useful estimation method. The Euler procedure is then applied to a stochastic interest rate process with mean reversion. This discrete time method is employed to estimate the dynamic process of the monthly US- T-bill rate with mean reversion where, however, the mean is allowed to undergo changes depending on long term interest rates. The time series data employed are from 1960.1 to 1995.1. In addition sub-periods are studied in order to find differences in the mean reverting behavior of the interest rate. As has been shown in Hsiao and Semmler (1999) although one can undertake continuous time estimations for such a process they are not always superior to the discrete time estimations using the Euler approximation. This encourages us to directly use the Euler approach in estimating the parameters of an interest rate process with mean reversion.

Recently it has become popular to define the short term interest rate process as a mean reverting process[4]. One could think that interest rates are generated from the following discrete time mean reverting process.

$$\Delta_h r_t = r_{t+h} - r_t = (\theta - \kappa r_t)h + \sigma \Delta_h B_t \qquad (2.8)$$

where B_t is one-dimensional Brownian motion and $\Delta_h B_t := B_{t+h} - B_t$ with h the time step.

The corresponding continuous time stochastic differential equation to (2.8) is:

---

[4]Several types of processes are discussed in the appendix and tested in Chan et al. (1992).

$$dr_t = (\theta - \kappa r_t)dt + \sigma dB_t \tag{2.9}$$

Note that both (2.8) and (2.9) represent a mean reverting process. We know that the solution to (2.9) is

$$r_t = e^{-\kappa t}(r_0 - \frac{\theta}{\kappa}(1 - e^{\kappa t}) + \sigma \int_0^t e^{\kappa s} dB_s) \tag{2.10}$$

One can generate data from using (2.8) "quasi-continuously" that means with an iteration time interval that is much finer than the observation intervals and we only take the data from the observation points. For the purpose of testing the usefulness of the Euler procedure this has been undertaken in Hsiao and Semmler (1999). There the Euler procedure has been tested against other alternatives, for example continuous time estimations. In our experiments the Ito integral represents the best approximation for our continuous time integral, yet, the continuous time estimation with primitive sums turns out to be better, for Ito's Lemma, see the Appendix 1. Since the discrete time Euler procedure is equivalent to taking primitive sums in the continuous time estimation we can conclude that the Euler method comes out best. Our hypothesis is therefore that the finer discreteness of the data does not add much independent information and thus does not give significantly better estimation results.[5] This seems to justify the use of the Euler procedure for discrete time estimations. Next, by employing the discrete time Euler procedure we undertake an estimation for actual data using a type of model such as represented by Eq. (2.8).

In fact a model as represented by Eq. (2.8) has often been employed for describing a mean reverting interest rate process, see Cox, Ingersoll and Ross (1985) and Balduzzi (1997).

A general mean reverting interest rate process with changing "central tendency" (Balduzzi 1997) can be written as follows:

$$dr = \kappa(\theta - r)dt + \sqrt{\sigma_0^2 + \sigma_1^2 r} dZ \tag{2.11}$$

$$\hat{\theta} = a_0 + a_1(B(\tau_2)\tau_1 y(\tau_1) - B(\tau_1)\tau_2 y(\tau_2)) \tag{2.12}$$

$$B(\tau) = \frac{2(e^{\delta \tau} - 1)}{(\lambda_1 + \delta + \kappa)(e^{\delta \tau} - 1) + 2\delta} \quad , \quad \delta = \sqrt{(\lambda_1 + \kappa)^2 + \sigma_1^2}$$

Assuming a stochastic process for θ such as $d\theta = m(\theta)dt + s(\theta)dW$.

Balduzzi (1997) takes $\hat{\theta}$ in (2.12) as an approximation of θ in (2.11). We use some assumptions to simplify the above model: (1) $\sigma_1^2 = 0$ and (2) δ is small.
Then

$$\delta = (\lambda_1 + \kappa)$$

$$B(\tau) = \frac{(1 - e^{-\delta \tau})}{(\lambda_1 + \kappa)}$$

---

[5]Balduzzi (1997) also employs the Euler discretization in his estimation strategy. He does not, however, give a justification for it.

When δ is small

$$e^{-\delta\tau} \sim 1 - \delta\tau$$

$$\Rightarrow B(\tau) = \frac{(1 - e^{-\delta\tau})}{(\lambda_1 + \kappa)} \sim \frac{(\delta\tau)}{(\lambda_1 + \kappa)}$$

$$\Rightarrow B(\tau_2)\tau_1 \sim B(\tau_1)\tau_2$$

then,

$$\hat{\theta} \sim a_0 + \tilde{a}_1(y(\tau_1) - y(\tau_2))$$

and

$$dr = (\kappa a_0 + \kappa\tilde{a}_1(y(\tau_1) - y(\tau_2)) - \kappa r)dt + \sigma_0 dZ$$
$$= (b_0 + b_1(y(\tau_1) - y(\tau_2)) + b_2 r)dt + \sigma_0 dZ \qquad (2.13)$$

Model (2.13) is linear in the variables. We use the following data:[6]

r_t : short-term interest rate, US monthly T-bill rate, annualized

$y(\tau_1)$: long-term interest rate, US T-bonds, constant maturity, 1YR

$y(\tau_2)$: long-term interest rate, US T-bonds, constant maturity, 3YR

All data employed are monthly data. Estimations are undertaken with non-linear least square estimation (NLLS). We use the AIC (Akaike Information Criterion) for evaluating the estimation results without and with long-term interest rate effect on the expected short-term interest rate. The AIC is computed as:

$$\ln \hat{\sigma}^2 + 2\frac{k}{n}$$

where k = number of parameters, n = number of observations.

Table 2.1. Parameter estimates without and with long-term rates

Period	AIC	
	$b_1 \neq 0$	$b_1 = 0$
Jan. 1960–Jun.1993	-1.132	-1.141
Sep. 1971–Sep. 1978	-1.671	-1.660
Oct. 1978–Sep. 1982	0.149	0.447
Oct. 1982–Jun. 1993	-2.575	-2.590

The term $b_1 \neq 0$ stands for the regression with the additional variable $y(\tau_1) - y(\tau_2)$ composed of the two long term rates and $b_1 = 0$ for the regression without the long

---

[6]The data are from Citibase (1998).

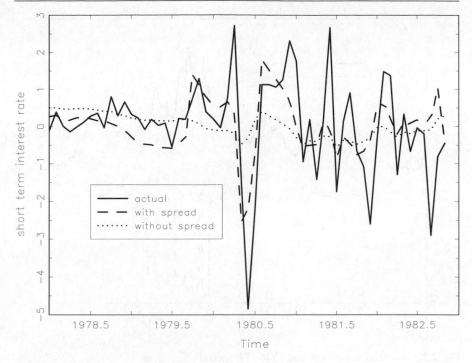

Fig. 2.1. Estimated time period 1978.1–1982.1

term rates. The regression with the lower AIC is always the significant result. As can be observed for the periods 1960.1–1993.6, with changes in the central tendency somewhere in the entire time period, the additional variable $y(\tau_1) - y(\tau_2)$ representing the two interest rates has no additional explanatory power. In shorter periods with stronger mean change the term $y(\tau_1) - y(\tau_2)$ has explanatory power. The latter holds for the period 1971–1978 and 1978–1982.

The first period is characterized by the end of the Bretton Woods system and the first oil crisis and the second by a strong change of the interest rate due to monetary policy of the Fed. This confirms that a time varying mean seems to become a relevant explanatory factor when trends in the interest rate change. Information on the changing mean can be extracted from the spread between the two long rates. In Fig. 2.1 the dotted line represents the regression without the interest rate spread and the dashed line represents the fitted line using interest spread. As the Fig. 2.1 shows the time period 1978.1–1982.1 is better tracked when the interest rate spread has become the significant additional explanatory variable.

In Fig. 2.2 it is also shown the 1YR-3YR spread. As the Fig. 2.2 indicates there is significant information in the 1YR-3YR spread when the mean of the short rate strongly moves during the time period 1978.1–1982.1.

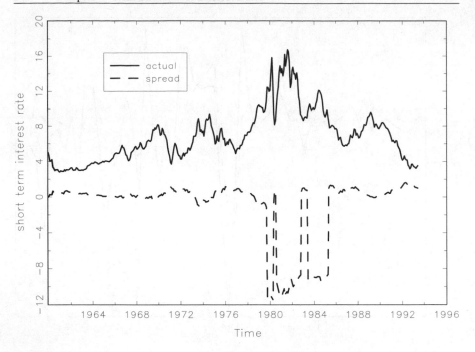

Fig. 2.2. Short-term interest rate and 1YR-3YR spread

2.4 Conclusions

A standard view on the term structure of interest rates is that the term structure can
be inferred from expected future short term interest rates. Our experiment has shown
that the discrete time Euler estimation appears to be a useful estimation method. The
Euler procedure is used for the estimation of the stochastic interest rate process with
mean reversion. Econometric regression studies on the term structure of interest rates
have frequently used information on longer term rates to forecast future short term
rates. Examples of this approach can be found in Fama (1984), Fama and Bliss (1987),
Mankiw (1996) and Campbell and Shiller (1992). Following Balduzzi (1997) we in
particular assume that longer maturity bond yields incorporate useful information
about the central tendency of the short term rate. We propose, however, a simplified
version of the more complex model by Balduzzi (1997) who allows for an additional
stochastic process to determine the central tendency. In our case the mean reversion
process is simply determined by the spread between two long rates. We show that the
spread between two longer maturity bond rates gives, for periods of stronger changes
of the central tendency, useful predictions for future short term rate movements and
thus for the term structure of interest rates.

Part II

The Credit Market and Economic Activity

Chapter 3
Theories on Credit Market, Credit Risk
and Economic Activity

3.1 Introduction

The next part deals with the credit market, credit market risk and economic activity. Historically, borrowing and lending have been considered essential for economic activity. The major issues in borrowing and lending theory were already present in the works of the classical economists such as Adam Smith, David Ricardo and Alfred Marshall. The Ricardian equivalence theorem, a modern reformulation of a statement by David Ricardo, has, in the theory of perfect capital markets, become a major issue in modern finance. We will discuss the theory of perfect capital markets and imperfect capital markets. In the latter, asymmetric information, moral hazard and adverse selection as well as asset prices become relevant issues for studying borrowing and lending. Subsequently, this will be applied to the finance of firms, households, governments and countries.

3.2 Perfect Capital Markets:
Infinite Horizon and Two Period Models

With the extension of perfect competition and general equilibrium theory to the intertemporal decisions of economic agents, studies of borrowing and lending have, thus, often been based on the theory of perfect capital markets (see Modigliani and Miller 1958, Blanchard and Fischer 1989, Chap. 2.).[1] In those multi period models the intertemporal budget constraint of economic agents (households, firms, government and countries) and, often, the so called transversality conditions are employed to make a statement on the solvency of the agents. These mean that the spending of agents can temporarily be greater than their income, and the agents can temporarily borrow against future income with no restriction, but an intertemporal budget constraint has to hold. This sometimes is also called the No-Ponzi condition and represents a statement on the non-explosiveness of the debt of an economic agent. Positing that the agents can borrow against future income, the non-explosiveness condition is, in fact, equivalent to the requirement that the intertemporal budget constraint holds for the

---

[1]The Modigliani-Miller Theorem means first that corporate leverage, the debt to equity ratio, does not matter for the value of the firm and second that it is irrelevant whether the firm or the share holders do the savings (the firm is a "veil" which acts on behalf of the share holders).

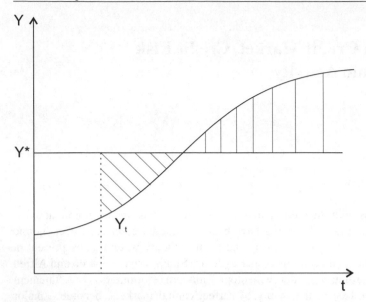

Fig. 3.1. Perfect capital market

agents. More precisely, this means that agents can borrow against future income but the discounted future income, the wealth of the agents, should be no smaller than the debt that agents have incurred. Indeed, models of this type have been discussed in the literature of households, firms, governments and small open economies (with access to international capital markets). Here, the transversality condition is a statement on the debt capacity of the agents.[2]

Figure 3.1 illustrates the idea of the perfect capital market. The economic agent can borrow when the income, Y_t, falls short of the normal spending, Y^*. In the long run, however, the segment below the horizontal line should be cancelled out by the segment above the horizontal line. This means that the future (discounted) surplus should be able to pay back the debt incurred.

On the other hand, in practice and as mentioned in the introduction, frequently economists assume an imperfect capital market by positing that borrowing is constrained. Either borrowing ceilings are assumed, agents supposedly preventing from borrowing an unlimited amount, or it is posited that borrowers face an upward sloping supply schedule for debt arising from a risk dependent interest rate. In the first case agents' assets are posited to serve as collateral. A convenient way to define the debt ceiling is to assume it is a fraction of the agents' wealth.[3] The risk dependent interest rate, it is frequently assumed is composed of a market interest rate (for ex-

---

[2]For a brief survey of such models for households, firms and governments or countries, see Blanchard and Fischer (1989, Chap. 2) and Turnovsky (1995).

[3]The definition of debt ceilings have become standard in models for small open economies; see, Barro, Mankiw and Sala-i-Martin (1995). It has also been pointed out that banks (like the

ample, an international interest rate) and an idiosyncratic component determined by the individual degree of risk of the borrower. Various forms of the agent specific risk premium can be assumed. Frequently, it is posited to be convex in the agents' debt[4] but it may be decreasing with the agents' own capital i.e. that capital which is serving as collateral for the loan.

We will return to borrowing and lending in imperfect capital markets, but, even in the context of the theory of perfect capital markets, one can argue that the non-explosiveness condition may pose some problems. In fact the No-Ponzi condition is state constrained and one has to show the regions where debt is feasible and the borrower remains creditworthy. In Semmler and Sieveking (1998, 1999) and Grüne, Semmler and Sieveking (2002) it is demonstrated that the debt ceiling should not be arbitrarily defined. When studying the debt capacity of the economic agent we can refer to a maximum amount that agents can borrow. Of course, in practice insolvency of the borrower can arise without the borrower moving up to his or her borrowing capacity. One should be interested in the maximum debt capacity up to which cred-itworthiness is preserved. Insolvency may occur when a borrower faces a loss of his or her "reputational collateral" (Bulow and Rogoff 1989) without having reached the debt capacity. In our view we should be concerned with the "ability to pay" and less with the borrower's "willingness to pay". Recent developments in the latter type of literature, in particular on the problem of incentive compatible contracts is surveyed in Eaton and Fernandez (1995). Rrecent studies of financial crises appear to pursue the line of ability to pay rather than the willingness to pay.

By undertaking such debt studies, we can often bypass utility theory. Economists have argued that analytical results in models with utility maximizing agents depend on the form of the utility function employed. Moreover, one can argue, economic theory should not necessarily be founded on the notion of utility since such a foundation is not well supported by empirical analysis. Many economists have recently argued that economic theory should refrain from postulating unobservables and employ observ-able variables as much as possible. We indeed want to argue that a theory of credit risk and creditworthiness, can be formulated without the use of utility theory.[5]

3.2.1 Infinite Horizon Model

Let us make some formal statements in the context of the theory of perfect capital markets. In a contract between a creditor and debtor there are two measurement problems involved. The first pertains to the computation of debt and the second to the computation of the debt ceiling. The first problem is usually answered by employing an equation of the form

---

World Bank, see, e.g. Bhandari, Haque and Turnovsky 1990) often define debt ceilings for their borrowers.

[4] The interest rate as function of the default risk of the borrower is posited by Bhandari, Haque and Turnovsky (1990) and Turnovsky (1995).

[5] An analytical treatment why and under what conditions the creditworthiness problem can be separated from the problem of the utility of consumption is given in Semmler and Sieveking (1998).

$$\dot{B}_t = rB_t - f_t, \tag{3.1}$$

where $B(t)$ is the level of debt[6] at time t, r the interest rate and $f(t)$ the net income. The second problem can be settled by defining a debt ceiling such as

$$B_t < B^*, \quad (t > 0)$$

or less restrictively by

$$\sup_{t \geq 0} B_t < \infty$$

or even less restrictively by the aforementioned transversality condition

$$\lim_{t \to \infty} e^{-rt} B_t = 0.$$

The latter condition, which represents the often used transversality condition, means that in the limit the debt should grow no faster than the discount rate which we have taken here as equal to the interest rate, r.

The ability of a debtor to service the debt, i.e. the feasibility of a contract, will depend on the debtors source of income, or more simply given the interest rate, r, on

$$\dot{B} = r B_t - (y_t - y^*)$$

where the transversality condition should hold:

$$\lim_{t \Rightarrow \infty} e^{-rt} B_t = 0.$$

The latter condition means that the debt, B_o, incurred by the economic agent will have to be paid off by the discounted future surplus, S_t.

$$B_t = B_o - \int_{t=0}^{\infty} e^{-rt} S_t dt = 0; \text{ where } S_t = y_t - y^*. \tag{3.2}$$

In an economic model with borrowing and lending[7] one can model this source of income as arising from production activity and thus from a stock of capital k_t, at time t, which changes with investment rate j_t at time t through

$$\dot{k}_t = j_t - \sigma k_t. \tag{3.3}$$

where k, capital stock, j_t, investment, and σk_t, depreciation. Our theory of credit and credit risk says that the debt capacity of a borrower is limited by a critical curve for each initial unit of capital stock, $k(0) = k_0$. Solvency of the agents and thus the case of no-bankruptcy is established for debt, B_0, below that critical debt curve.

This is shown in the figure below; for details see Semmler and Sieveking (1998, 1999).

---

[6]Note that all subsequent state variables are written in terms of efficiency labor along the line of Blanchard (1983).

[7]Prototype models used as basis for our further presentation can be found in Blanchard (1983), Blanchard and Fischer (1989) or Turnovsky (1995).

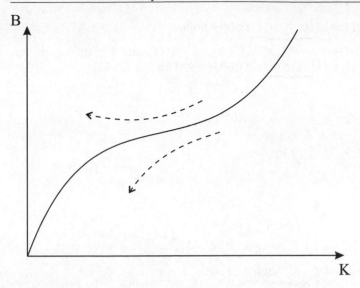

Fig. 3.2. Critical debt curve

This is likely to mean that the agent will be cut off from loans if he or she approaches the critical curve and, moreover, loans might be recalled. An empirical study on debt sustainability using the intertemporal budget constraint is given in Chap. 4.4.

For a country such a debt constraint means that once the critical level of debt is reached there will be a sudden reversal of capital flows, possibly triggering an exchange rate devaluation or exchange rate crisis that is possibly followed by a financial crisis and large output loss. Further details of the study of such a process triggered by credit risk and insolvency threat are postponed to Chap. 12.

3.2.2 A Two Period Model

A two period model for households, firms, states and countries can be found in Burda and Wyplosz (1997, Chap. 3). We see that even without an initial value of debt, the problem of sustainability of debt already arises in a two period model. This is shown below.

Borrowing and Lending in a two-period model reads as follows. In the first period there are two possibilities

$$y_1 - c_1 \begin{cases} a) \ y_1 > c_1 \Rightarrow \text{lending (see point M)} \\ b) \ y_1 < c_1 \Rightarrow \text{borrowing (see point P)} \end{cases}$$

whereby c_1 = first period consumption and y_1 = first period income. With c_2 = second period consumption and y_2 = second period income we have for the second period

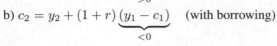

a) $c_2 = y_2 + (1 + r)\underbrace{(y_1 - c_1)}_{>0}$ (with lending)

b) $c_2 = y_2 + (1 + r)\underbrace{(y_1 - c_1)}_{<0}$ (with borrowing)

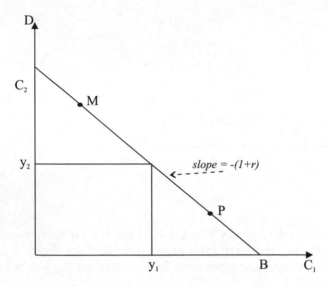

Fig. 3.3. Two period model

The intertemporal budget constraint (IBC) for a two period model can be derived as follows: From $c_2 = y_2 + (y_1 - c_1)(1 + r)$ we obtain in terms of the present value of next period's income and consumption: $c_1 + \frac{c_2}{1+r} = y_1 + \frac{y_2}{1+r}$.

The IBC with initial wealth (V_0) reads:

$$c_1 + \frac{c_2}{1+r} = y_1 + \frac{y_2}{1+r} + V_0$$

The IBC with initial debt (B_0) reads:

$$c_1 + \frac{c_2}{1+r} = y_1 + \frac{y_2}{1+r} - B_0$$

and

$$B_0^* = \underbrace{\underbrace{y_1 + \frac{y_2}{1+r}}_{\text{income}} - \underbrace{(c_1 + \frac{c_2}{1+r})}_{\text{consumption}}}_{\text{net wealth}}$$

or

B_0^* − net wealth = 0

Thus, in this latter case the initial value of debt, B_0, is not allowed to be greater then the critical debt B_0^* which is equal to the value of net wealth.

Thus in a two period model sustainable debt is

$$B_0^* = V_2 = y_1 + \frac{y_2}{1+r} - \left(c_1 + \frac{c_2}{1+r}\right). \tag{3.4}$$

If $V_2 < B_0$ then the agent has lost creditworthiness and bankruptcy occurs. This is graphically presented in the following figure.

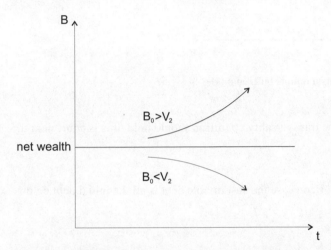

Fig. 3.4. Creditworthiness in a two period model

In the infinite horizon case $(t \to \infty)$ we have as the present value:

$$V_t = \int_{t=0}^{\infty} e^{-rt} S_t dt$$

where $S_t = y_t - y^*$ (for one period).

The IBC with initial debt (B_0) reads:

$$B_0^* = \int_{t=0}^{\infty} e^{-rt} S_t dt$$

$$B_t = B_0 - \int_{t=0}^{\infty} e^{-rt} S_t dt.$$

The right hand side is the remaining debt. The law of motion for debt is:

$$\dot{B} = r B_t - S_t .$$

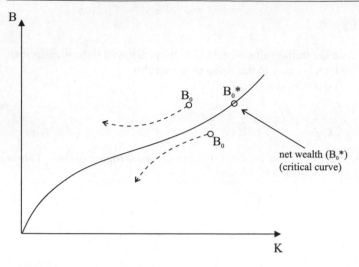

Fig. 3.5. Creditworthiness in an infinite horizon model

If it is required that the transversality condition should hold, this is equivalent to

$$\lim_{t \Rightarrow \infty} e^{-rt} B_t = 0$$

Thus, in the infinite horizon case the sustainable debt is all the initial debt below the curve in Fig. 3.5.

If

$$B_0 > \int_0^\infty e^{-rt} S_t dt \tag{3.5}$$

there is a loss of creditworthiness and thus bankruptcy will occur; for details see Semmler and Sieveking (1998, 1999).

In Chap. 4.4 we employ a small scale model to demonstrate how an income stream may be generated through a production activity and a process of capital accumulation. There we will also show how debt sustainability can be empirically estimated.

The theory of imperfect capital markets suggests practical rules on how to deal with credit risk and the loss of creditworthiness. Two rules are typically imposed on borrowers. First, there will be credit rationing and debt ceilings. In a two period case there might be a borrowing constraint introduced such that there is credit rationing whereby a debt ceiling, B_2, is given by: $B_2 \leq B_0^* = V_2$ (net wealth). In the infinite horizon case credit rationing and debt ceiling might be given by: $B_0 \leq B_0^* = \int_{t=0}^\infty e^{-rt} S_t dt$.

Second, there may be endogenous credit costs wherein the interest payment depends on the debts and assets (or net worth) of the economic agents. One could, for example, introduce an equation for the evolution of debt such as

$$\dot{B} = H(k, B)B_t - S_t \tag{3.6}$$

wherein $H(k, B)$ is the endogenous credit cost with S_t the net income flow, see Chaps. 4.4 and 12.[8]

3.3 Imperfect Capital Markets: Some Basics

Next we will work out details of the theory of imperfect capital markets, both on the level of agents' actions as well as on the aggregate level. An excellent presentation of the theory of imperfect capital markets is given by Jaffee and Stiglitz (1990). There, the notion of asymmetric information is essential which gives the theory of credit contract a realistic feature. Indeed, credit markets differ from standard markets (e.g. for cars, consumer goods) in some important respects. First, standard markets, which are the focus of classical competitive theory, involve a number of agents who are buying and selling an homogenous commodity. Second, in standard markets, the delivery of a commodity by a seller and payment for the commodity by a buyer occur simultaneously. This is different for credit contracts.

Credit received today by an individual or firm involves a promise of repayment sometime in the future. Yet, one person's promise is different from the promise of another and promises are frequently broken. It is difficult to determine the likelihood that a promise will be kept. Given the little information the lender has about the borrower, moral hazard and adverse selection may indeed affect the likelihood of loan repayment. For most entrepreneurial investment the project is always specific. Credit means allocating resources but those who control existing resources, or have claims on current wealth, are not necessarily those best situated to use these resources. On the other hand, the user of the resource has specific information.

The analysis of credit allocation may go wrong when we apply the standard supply and demand model which is not totally appropriate for the market for promises. If credit markets were like standard markets, then interest rates would be the "prices" that equate the demand and supply for credit. However, an excess demand for credit is common – applications for credit are frequently not granted. As a result, the demand for credit may exceed the supply at the market interest rate. Credit markets deviate from the standard model because the interest rate indicates only what the individual promises to repay, not what he or she will actually repay. This means that credit markets are not necessarily cleared since the interest rate is not the only dimension of a credit contract. Given the above informational and collateral problems in borrowing and lending in principle there should be a different cost of credit for each economic agent.

As Jaffee and Stiglitz (1990) notice, in most advanced countries complicated, decentralized, and interrelated set of financial markets, institutions, and instruments have evolved to provide credit. We here, focus on loan contracts where the promised

---

[8]For further details, see Semmler and Sieveking (1998, 1999), see also Bernanke, Gertler and Gilchrist (1998).

repayments are fixed amounts. "At the other extreme, equity securities are promises to repay a given fraction of a firm's income. A spectrum of securities, including convertible bonds and preferred shares, exists between loans and equity. Each of these securities provides for the exchange of a current resource for a future promise. In our discussion we shall uncover a number of "problems" with the loan market. While some of these problems are addressed by other instruments, these other instruments have their own problems" (Jaffee and Stiglitz 1990:838).

The problem of the allocation of credit has important implications at both the micro and macro levels. At the micro level, in the absence of a credit market, those with resources would have to invest the resources themselves, possibly receiving a lower return than could be obtained by others. When credit is allocated poorly, inferior investment projects are undertaken, and the nation's resources are misguided. "Credit markets, of course, do exist, but they may not function well – or at least they may not function as would a standard market – in allocating credit. The special nature of credit markets is most evident in the case of credit rationing, where borrowers are denied credit even though they are willing to pay the market interest rate (or more), while apparently similar borrowers do obtain credit" (Jaffee and Stiglitz 1990:839).

At the macroeconomic level, changes in credit allocations are strongly connected with economic fluctuations and often also with rapid decline in productive activities. For example, the disruption of bank lending during the early 1930s may have created, or at least greatly extended, the Great Depression of the 1930s. Moreover, financial and credit crises have contributed to the Mexican (1994), Asian (1997–1998) and Russian (1998) economic crises. The availability of credit may also strongly be affected by monetary policy. Central banks often provide new liquidity when the financial system is disrupted (e.g. October 1987). Another example is that the Fed often has used credit crunches – enforced credit rationing – to slow down an overheating economy. In fact, as already indicated in Chap. 2, monetary policy effectively works through the credit channel and thus the credit institutions transmit monetary policy shocks; for more details see Chap. 11.

Differences between promised and actual repayments on loans, or even the default of loans, are the result of uncertainty concerning the borrower's ability to make repayments when due. On the other hand, the lender may not be willing to pay and/or deliver the funds to other users. Both the ability or willingness to pay creates the risk of default for the lender. Some aspects of uncertainty may be treated with the standard model, as illustrated by the capital asset pricing model or other models where there is a fixed and known probability of default. The capital asset pricing model will be taken up in Chap. 8.

Given that borrowers and lenders may have different access to information concerning a project's risk, they may evaluate risk differently. In words of Jaffee and Stiglitz one can refer "to symmetric information as the case in which borrowers and lenders have equal access to all available information. The opposite case – which we will call generically imperfect information – has many possibilities. Asymmetrical information, where the borrower knows the expected return and risk of his project, whereas the lender knows only the expected return and risk of the average project in the economy, is a particularly important case. Uncertainty regarding consumer and (risky) government loans can be described with the same format used for firms, although, of course, the underlying sources of uncertainty are different" (Jaffee and Stiglitz 1990:840).

Next, let us undertake a more formal presentation. Details of such an exposition can be found in Jaffee and Stiglitz (1990). Most of the subsequent elaborations for the micro as well as macro levels are supposed to hold for one period zero horizon models.

3.4 Imperfect Capital Markets: Microtheory

Let us elaborate some elements of the theory of imperfect capital markets. A credit contract involves the relation between a creditor and a borrower.

The first important element in this relation is that of asymmetric information. The borrower knows for what purpose the loan will be used, but the lender is less informed about the use of the loan. The borrower promises to pay back the loan with interest. The lender faces heterogenous agents and each borrower's promise is different. The risk of not getting the loan back depends on the borrower's willingness to pay ability. In the last section, we discussed the ability to pay. A risk for the lender may, however, also arise if the borrower has some incentives not to pay. This concerns the willingness to pay by the borrower.[9] In recent credit market theories this has been discussed under the topic of incentive compatible debt contracts.[10]

The problem of the ability to pay for the one period zero horizon case can be formalized as follows. Let there be two possible outcomes for the project of the borrower, x^a and x^b, whereby $x^a > x^b$ and x^a = good result; x^b = bad result. Let p^a, p^b be the probability of the occurrence of x^a, x^b; with $p^a + p^b = 1$. Then we have the expectations: $x^e = p^a x^a + p^b x^b$.

With this notation we describe the second important element in modern debt contracts. This is the limited liability of the borrower which can be described in the following scheme with B the loan and r the interest rate:

creditor $\leftarrow (1+r) B$ from borrower

(i) $x^b < (1+r) B$ (bad result)

(ii) $x^b < (1+r) B < x^a$ (good result).

In the second case, since $x^a > x^b$, the borrower's gain is $x^a - (1+r) B$. Thus, in case there is a good outcome, x^a, the borrower has a gain. Note that limited liability refers to the bad outcome where the borrower is not liable for the loss. The creditor would thus be inclined to require a collateral so as to cover the potential loss. A

---

[9]Consider for example the case of a sovereign borrower whose value of the debt is B and M is the value of the access to the capital market. Then if sovereign debt B>M the debtor might not be willing to pay.

[10]For this line of research, see Townsend (1979) and Bernanke and Gertler (1989).

collateral of the borrower promised to be transferred to the creditor in case of a loss, could be of the following type of asset: liquid funds, financial assets or physical capital. Yet, note that in most cases the value of collateral is uncertain.

On the other hand, the creditor may grant credit but charge for different types of borrowers a different interest rate because different borrowers have different risk characteristics (that require different risk rates). So we may have r_1 for the risky borrower and r_2 for the less risky borrower with $r_1 > r_2$.

A third important element in modern credit markets is rationing of loans. If borrowers have desired loans of L^* and the creditor offers loans of the amount L there are two cases: (1) if $L < L^*$ (desired loans), the interest rate the borrower offers may increase and we get L=L*. In this case no rationing would occur. (2) the borrowers do not receive loans in case even if they offer an interest rate $r^* > r$. Pure credit rationing of credits might occur only for few borrowers, although all potential borrowers are assumed to be equal.

The question is why the creditor is not interested in granting a loan even at a higher interest rate. Why is there usually a disequilibrium in the credit market? Consider a modern banking sector that receives deposits and gives loans to the public (firms or households)

Assets	Liabilities
R (reserves)	D (deposits)
L (loans)	r (interest)

The banking sector could be competitive or there could be, because of a limited number of banks, oligopolistic or monopolistic behavior in the offering of loans. In any case, one can usually observe the following disequilibrium in the credit market.

The reasons for this are as follows. There is the expected rate of return of the bank and there are interest rates offered by borrowers. Yet, with increasing "default" probability, with higher interest rates offered by the borrower, the banks face higher loan losses. In particular, this occurs if there is adverse selection, i.e. that means if the proportion of riskier borrowers increases when r rises.

A profit maximizing bank will, as shown in Fig. 3.7, restrict loans, since its return will not increase even if borrowers offer a higher interest rate.

Therefore, there is usually excess demand for loans: $Q^D > Q^S$ as shown in Fig. 3.6.

Note that with a default risk of the borrower the profit of the bank is:

$$\pi = \xi (1 + r) B - (1 + \delta) B \tag{3.7}$$

where ξ is the percent of repaid loans and δ the interest rate that the bank has to pay. This results in the "required" rate of return by banks

$$1 + r^* = \frac{(1 + \delta)}{\xi}$$

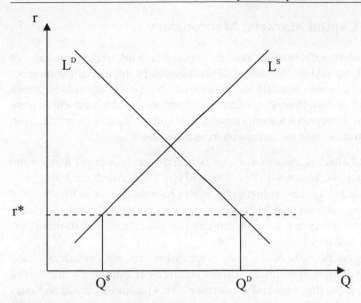

Fig. 3.6. Disequilibrium in the loan market

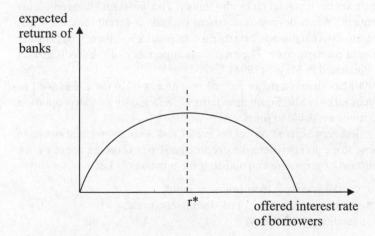

Fig. 3.7. Profit maximizing bank

Here we assume that banks of profit are zero in a competitive banking system. The bank could, however, in order to find out the quality of the borrower suggest the following alternative debt contracts to the borrower: a debt contract with collateral or higher interest rate. The borrower's choice reveals information to the bank about a quality of the borrower.

3.5 Imperfect Capital Markets: Macrotheory

The above theory of imperfect capital markets is based on work in the economics of information by Stiglitz and his co-authors. This has greatly influenced the macroe-conomic modelling of credit markets and economic activity. We again look at one period zero horizon models. Here asymmetric information, moral hazard and adverse selection as well as asset prices are important. From various studies on credit, asset prices and production activity we can summarize three major results:

1. asymmetric information induces a wedge between costs of internal finance and external finance (see Townsend 1979, 1984, Myers 1984, Auerbach 1984)
2. There is an implied a financial hierarchy where internal finance is the cheapest way of financing investment, debt finance is more expensive and equity finance is the most expensive way to finance investment (see Greenwald and Stiglitz 1993, Bernanke and Gertler 1989), see Fig. 3.8.
3. the cost of capital depends on the asset price of the firm, i.e. "collaterals" and balance sheets of firms. Investment exhibits an inverse relationship to the cost of capital giving rise to the "financial accelerator". This means that credit and asset prices accelerate the down turn of the economy but also accelerate the upturn. [11]

Figure 3.8 illustrates the financial hierarchy theory. The horizontal line represents the desired investment. When desired investment exceeds a certain amount firms switch from internal to external finance, first using debt finance and then, when further investment is required equity finance. The empirical importance of the credit market for investment is illustrated in Mayer (1991).[12]

As Mayer (1990) has shown a major part of investment is, in the US as well as other countries, financed by credit. Equity financing is, in fact, only a small proportion of the financing options available to firms.

In a simple one period zero horizon model on credit and output some authors have illustrated the above three points where the credit cost depends on the agency cost. This represents the cost of screening and auditing the borrower.[13] Let

$k_i(\pi_i)$: units of capital goods; q: their price; x: input

π_i: probability of state i occurring; r : risk-free interest rate;

S^e: collateral; p: auditing probability.

---

[11] In earlier literature the procyclical effects of credit were already known. Marshall, for example, states: "As credit by growing makes itself grow, so when distrust has taken the place of confidence, failure and panic breed panic and failure" (Marshall) cited in Boyd and Blatt (1988). A similar statement can be found in Minsky: "Success breeds a disregard of the possibility of failures the absence of serious financial difficulties over a substantial period leads .... to a euphoric economy in which short-term financing of long-term positions become a normal way of life. As a previous financial crisis recedes in time, it is quite natural for central bankers, government officials, bankers, businessmen, and even economists to believe that a new era has arrived." (Minsky 1986:213)

[12] For further data and figures, see Mayer (1991)

[13] See Bernanke and Gertler (1989) and Bernanke, Gertler and Gilchrist (1998) for a multiperiod model.

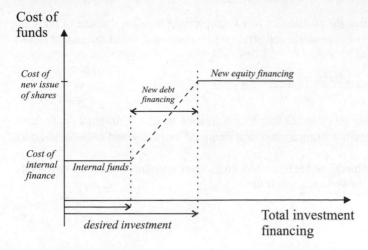

Fig. 3.8. Financial hierarchy

We assume for a bad state: $i = 1$; and for a good state: $i = 2$. Firms borrow from creditors the amount $x - S^e$. The outcome of the production activity could be

$$qk_i(\pi_i) \lessgtr (1 + r)(x - S^e).$$

But note that the risk-free interest rate, r, does not represent yet the total borrowing cost. There is an additional agency cost (the cost of screening and auditing) which is

$$\pi_1 p(S^e)q\gamma \quad \text{where} \quad p_{S^e} < 0, \gamma > 0.$$

Borrowers will thus have to pay an external financing premium which mainly depends on their own equity. The external financing premium will be the lower the higher the internal equity of the borrower. This makes credit cost endogenous and agent specific, for details see Section 12.6.

We thus get the above main three results. First, premium cost for external finance is inversely related to S^e, the equity value of the firm. Second, there is a financing hierarchy. Third, investment is inversely related to premium cost (the lower the collateral the greater the cost of external finance). This gives rise to the financial accelerator. For the relevance of this theory for macroeconomics and for an empirical test of this theory, see Gertler et al. (1991), Bernanke and Gertler (1994) and Bernanke, Gertler and Gilchrist (1998).

Another model in the same vain has been presented by Greenwald and Stiglitz (1993). Take

y^n: net income; $Q(k)$: output; k: capital input;
P_B: probability of bankruptcy; D: debt; b_o : the entrepreneur's own fund.

Then we may write $y^n = Q(k) - (1 + r)(k - b_o) - cP_B$

By assuming that the probability of bankruptcy depends on the size of the loan (which is assumed in Greenwald and Stiglitz to be proportional to the capital stock) we thus have:

$$Q' = (1 + r) + c\frac{\partial P_B}{\partial k}; \left(c\frac{\partial P_B}{\partial k} > 0\right).$$

This theory also gives us the same three results as above. Internal funds have lower cost than external finance, there is a financial hierarchy and lastly credit may be procyclical.

A multi-period model on the relation of finance and investment has been developed by Fazzari et al. (1988). It reads as follows:

$$V_{\max} = \int_0^\infty \left(\pi_t - (1 + \Omega_t)V_t^N\right)e^{-\rho t}dt \tag{3.8}$$

where π_t are profit flows, V_t^N the new equity issue, ρ the discount rate, and Ω_t the premium cost for external finance. Here, too, the hierarchy of finance and the inverse relation of financial risk (default risk) and investment can be derived. Fazzari et al. (1988) also undertake an empirical test of the theory by regressing the investment on cash flows of firms for size classes of firms. Smaller firms are more likely to be credit constrained and thus their relation of cash flow and investment is expected to be strongest.

Another model with borrowing and lending and imperfect capital market is presented in Blanchard (1983). In his model, there is an effect of debt on the utility of households, for example, of a country that borrows:

$$V_{\max} = \int_0^\infty U\left(c_t - G(b_t)\right)e^{-\rho t}dt \qquad\qquad G' > 0, G'' \geq 0 \tag{3.9}$$

s.t

$$\dot{k} = i_t - \delta k_t$$
$$\dot{b} = rb + \left(c + i(1 + \varphi(i/k)) - f(k)\right)$$

with δ the depreciation rate of capital. The latter equation represents the debt dynamics with $f(k)$ a production function, investment, i and adjustment cost of capital, $\varphi(i/k)$. All variables are written in efficiency units, with c, consumption, k, capital stock, b, debt and $G(b)$, disutility of debt.

The Blanchard model includes the cost of debt in the utility functions. A variant of the Blanchard model will be discussed further below, see Chap. 4.4.

3.6 Imperfect Capital Markets: The Micro-Macro Link

The above models on imperfect capital markets and real activity – on the micro as well as macro level – mostly use a framework with one period and zero time horizon.

A few exceptions that use an intertemporal framework were also briefly discussed. Next we want to present a model that shows the micro-macro link in an intertemporal framework. The model is based on Uzawa (1968) and is taken up in Asada and Semmler (1995). This model explores in particular the impact of debt on the asset price of the firm. Whereas the former is still in the tradition of perfect capital markets, the latter explicitly takes imperfect capital markets into account.

In the standard model the capital market and thus finance does not really matter for the activity of the firm. The capital structure is irrelevant for the present value of the firm and thus the optimal investment is independent of capital markets. This appears as a common feature of prototype infinite horizon models of the firm. Since the finance of the firm's investment is nonessential, the model disregards an explicit specification of the evolution of the capital structure. Along the lines of Modigliani and Miller (1958), it is usually demonstrated that neither the type of equity financing (financing through retained earnings or issuance of new equity) nor the capital structure matter for the value of the firm and thus for investment. A kind of separation theorem holds, according to which decisions on investment are independent from financing practices and thus, the debt dynamics of the firm.

Equivalent results hold in models where a representative household's utility is maximized over time. The objective function of the firm is here replaced by a utility function. Formally, for example, in Blanchard and Fisher (1989: 58) a system with two state variables representing the evolution of capital stock and a debt equation, depicting the household's evolution of debt can be introduced. Here, too, if debt has no impact on consumption or investment behaviors, finance becomes irrelevant for optimal consumption, investment, and output. In fact, for the system's solution, one can disregard the evolution of debt (Blanchard and Fisher 1989: 63).

It was the development of the economics of information, as discussed in the previous sections, that led to the development of intertemporal models with imperfect capital markets. The above theory, as put forward by Stiglitz and others, for example, has initiated a change of perspective on finance and economic activity. The essential point for intertemporal models is that bankruptcy or default risk arising from the firm's financial structure may result in cross-effects between the real and financial sides and thus finance and financial structure matter for real activity. In this context, then, a second state equation representing the financial structure of the firm becomes relevant for the growth path of the firm, as does the financial hierarchy theory as aforementioned. When the debt burden of the firm and the associated probability of bankruptcy or default risk are present, the present value of the firm and investment are affected. This gives us the micro-macro link in intertemporal models that we are seeking.

There appear to be many variations of how bankruptcy risk affects the present value of the firm and thus investment in imperfect capital markets. All of them admit cross effects. More formally, we can distinguish three approaches that admit such cross effects.

In a first view, it is postulated that there is a unique relationship between the risk of the firm and the discount rate.[14] In fact, more formally, it can be shown that the discount rate is a monotonic increasing function of the risk a firm faces. In the limit when the discount rate approaches infinity, i.e. the risk approaches infinity, no resources are allocated to the future and a zero horizon optimization problem arises, see Sieveking and Semmler (1994). In general it is posited that the higher the risk of not receiving a cash flow next period, the lower investment.

A second view stresses that the bankruptcy or default risk will affect the value of the firm primarily through the cost arising from external finance, in particular, debt finance. The implicit cost of raising external funds is best summarized in a survey article by Myers: "Costs of financial distress include the legal and administrative costs of bankruptcy, as well as the subtler agency, moral hazard, monitoring and contracting costs which can erode firm value even if formal default is avoided" (Myers 1984: 581).[15] The cost of debt financed investments, resulting from a high leverage of the firm may have, as shown above, a direct (negative) effect on investment. In the models by Greenwald and Stiglitz (1993) the actual cost of raising external funds is a direct function of the debt the firm has incurred.[16] Along the line of the literature on adjustment costs of capital, the borrowing cost is hereby conceived to be a convex one.[17]

A third, more complete conception claims that risk or default cost will actually affect both the discount rate and the cost of external funds. The proposition that "the firm's riskiness increases with the degree of leverage" (Auerbach 1979: 438) can be translated into the view that the discount rate as well as the borrowing cost are a function of the degree of leverage.[18] Here it is often assumed that the interest rate is a convex function of the leverage. Although this line of thought represents the most comprehensive conception of how the firm's degree of leverage affects its value, it is analytically the least tractable formulation.

From all of the above three views one can conclude that a higher default risk of firms arising from debt finance will negatively covary with investment and output. We will summarize some results obtained by Asada and Semmler (1995) who followed the second view in an analytical study of such a dynamic model with credit markets.

---

[14]Non-constant discount rate models are increasingly discussed in modern finance theory. For further details on time varying or stochastic discount rates, see Chaps. 9–10. From an empirical perspective the discount rate is, however, rather unobservable. Therefore, proxies are now often used in econometric work for discount rates, see Shiller (1991, 2001).

[15]Note that the above formulation of the "cost of external finance" refers not solely to a higher interest rate for risky firms but rather to a whole set of factors eroding a firm's value. Also note that, as shown by Myers (1984), empirical tests on this matter are difficult to conduct.

[16]Greenwald and Stiglitz argue that the risk of bankruptcy depends on the firm's indebtedness. With debt service as a fixed obligation, the corresponding higher probability of bankruptcy is reflected in the value of the firm. As they argue, the financial market may reappraise the underlying probability of bankruptcy for firms with higher debt service.

[17]Auerbach (1984: 34) for example, states: "interest rate on debt .... is a convex, increasing function of the debt-capital ratio."

[18]For details, see Auerbach (1979).

It is analytically the most tractable one and gives empirical predictions akin to the other views. Since the third view is analytically rather untractable only simulation results can be obtained; see Asada and Semmler (1995).

The starting point for such a model with capital market is the Uzawa (1968) model. His variant without credit reads

$$V_{\max} = \int_0^\infty e^{-\rho t} \left(r_t - \varphi(g_t)\right) K_t dt \tag{3.10}$$

s.t.

$$\frac{\dot{K}_t}{K_t} = g_t$$

$$0 = \varphi(g_t)K_t - RP_t - \dot{E}_{pt}$$

whereby r is the rate of return on capital; φ = costs of investment; E_p= equity; RP= retained profit.

The explicit extension to a model of a monopolistic firm, still without credit, reads with E_t, effort, and, using the ratio $\frac{X_t}{K_t}$ (with X_t output and K_t capital stock)

$$\underset{E_t, g_t, s_{t_f}}{V_{\max}} = \int_0^\infty \left[\{p(E_t) - c\} E_t - \varphi(g_t)\right] K_t e^{-\rho t} dt \tag{3.11}$$

$$\dot{K} = g_t K_t; \qquad\qquad K_0 > 0 \tag{3.12}$$

$$\dot{d} = \varphi(g_t) - \left[\{p(E_t) - c\} E_t - i d_t\right] s_{t_f} - g_t d_t; \tag{3.13}$$

where c is the production cost; d_t the debt-capital stock ratio $\frac{D_t}{K_t}$; i the interest rate (constant); and ρ the discount rate.

The debt equation is derived from:

$$\frac{\dot{d}_t}{d_t} = \frac{\dot{D}_t}{D_t} - \frac{\dot{K}_t}{K_t} = \frac{\varphi(g_t)K_t - \left[\{p(E_t) - c\} E_t - i d_t\right] s_{t_f} K_t}{D_t} - g_t.$$

In this set up, as Asada and Semmler (1995) have shown the credit market has no effect on the value of the firm. The fact that the firm finances its investment through loans from the capital markets does not matter either. Finance and investment are still separated as in Modigliani and Miller (1958).

Next we introduce a feedback effect of debt finance on the value of the monopolistic firm.

$$\underset{E_t, g_t, s_{t_f}}{V_{\max}} = \int_0^\infty \left[\{p(E_t) - c\} E_t - \varphi_1(g_t) - \varphi_2(i d_t)\right] K_t e^{-\rho t} dt \tag{3.14}$$

$$\dot{K} = g_t K_t; \qquad\qquad K_0 > 0 \tag{3.15}$$

$$\dot{d} = \varphi_1(g_t) - \left[\{p(E_t) - c\} E_t - i d_t\right] s_{t_f} - g_t d_t; \tag{3.16}$$

where we can take

Table 3.1. Comparative static results

1.	$\rho \nearrow$ (discount rate)	$\Rightarrow$	$g^* \searrow$ ($d^* \searrow$)	rows $1-3$
2.	$\beta \nearrow$ (risk parameter)	$\Rightarrow$	$g^* \searrow$ ($d^* \searrow$	rows $4-6$
3.	$\eta \searrow$ (demand with low elasticity)	$\Rightarrow$	$g^* \nearrow$ ($d^* \nearrow$)	rows $7-9$
4.	$i \nearrow$ (interest rate)	$\Rightarrow$	$g^* \searrow$ ($d^* \searrow$)	rows 10–12
5.	$c \nearrow$ (costs)	$\Rightarrow$	$g^* \searrow$ ($d^* \searrow$)	rows 13–15
6.	$s_f \nearrow$ (self-financing)	$\Rightarrow$	$g^* \nearrow$ ($d^* \searrow$)	rows 16–18
7.	$B \searrow$ (reaction of demand to total demand)	$\Rightarrow$	$g^* \searrow$ ($d^* \searrow$)	rows 19–21
8.	$\alpha \nearrow$ (adjustment cost of capital)	$\Rightarrow$	$g^* \searrow$ ($d^* \searrow$)	rows 22–24

$$\varphi_1(g_t) = g_t + \alpha(g_t)^2, \ \alpha > 0$$
$$\varphi_2(0) = 0, \ \varphi_2'(id_t) > 0, \ \varphi_2''(id_t) > 0 \text{ for example}$$
$$\varphi_2(id_t) = \beta(id_t)^2, \ \beta > 0.$$

Hereby we have defined φ_1 the cost of investment and φ_2 the influence of bankruptcy risk on the firm value (convex).

The solution and the dynamics of the above model is studied in Asada and Semmler (1995) by using the Hamiltonian approach. It suffices to report the comparative static results. Herein an inverse demand function of the following type is assumed

$$X_t = A_t p_t^{-\eta} \Rightarrow X_t = BK_t p_t^{-\eta};$$

where $B > 0$ and $\eta > 1$ (elasticity of demand)

The inverse demand function is given by:

$$p_t = B^{\frac{1}{\eta}} E_t^{-\frac{1}{\eta}} = p(E_t) \tag{3.17}$$

From the necessary conditions for optimality using the Hamiltonian one obtains (for the control variables g, E and the state variables d, K and the co-state variables λ_1, λ_2) $g^*, d^*, E^* > 0$ (with s_f prespecified) and an equation for the price-cost margin

$$B^{\frac{1}{\eta}} E_t^{1-\frac{1}{\eta}} - cE_t = (p(E_t) - c) E_t = \frac{1}{\eta - 1} cE^*.$$

Table 3.2. Value of g^*, d^* and V^* for different parameter constellations

row	parameter	equilibrium values		
		g*	d*	V*
1.	$\rho = 0.12^*$	0.0486	0.122	13.46
2.	$\rho = 0.115$	0.0504	0.210	13.63
3.	$\rho = 0.1$	0.0589	0.588	12.79
4.	$\beta = 40$	0.0476	0.069	13.65
5.	$\beta = 20^*$	0.0486	0.122	13.46
6.	$\beta = 4$	0.0523	0.303	12.79
7.	$\eta = 5.35$	0.0262	-0.477	7.93
8.	$\eta = 4.35^*$	0.0486	0.122	13.46
9.	$\eta = 4.0$	0.0657	0.511	14.11
10.	$i = 0.06$	0.0473	0.061	13.71
11.	$i = 0.04^*$	0.0486	0.122	13.46
12.	$i = 0.02$	0.0520	0.257	12.85
13.	$c = 1.68$	0.0238	-0.557	6.90
14.	$c = 1.38^*$	0.0486	0.122	13.46
15.	$c = 1.28$	0.0706	0.616	13.82
16.	$s_f = 0.2$	0.0396	0.321	12.76
17.	$s_f = 0.3^*$	0.0486	0.122	13.46
18.	$s_f = 0.4$	0.0569	-0.020	13.84
19.	$B = 4.3$	0.0268	-0.457	8.20
20.	$B = 7.3^*$	0.0486	0.122	13.46
21.	$B = 10.3$	0.0842	0.903	11.98
22.	$\alpha = 7.5$	0.0658	0.503	10.95
23.	$\alpha = 11.5^*$	0.0486	0.122	13.46
24.	$\alpha = 15.5$	0.0416	-0.093	14.09

The latter, E*, is the steady state of E which is given by

$$E^* = \frac{(1 - \frac{1}{\eta})^\eta B}{c^\eta}.$$

The results on investment (growth rate of capital stock) and the debt to capital stock ratio can be reported from a comparative-static study of the above model (rows refer to Table 3.2):

Table 3.1 reports the parameters and the respective equilibrium values for the growth rates, the debt to capital stock ratios and the asset price of the firm.

Overall, the model predicts that investment (and thus the growth rate of capital) falls with higher discount rate, higher risk coefficient, higher interest rate, greater elasticity of demand, lower retention ratio and higher adjustment cost of capital. Those effects would in fact be expected from economic reasoning and studies on the determinants of firms' investment, growth and stock market value. On the other hand, as the model also shows in most cases, except for the case of declining self-financing, that the debt to capital stock ratio falls. These are steady state results and it thus might be reasonable as well to expect a lower debt to capital stock ratio for lower growth rates of the capital stock. Economic growth is accompanied by increasing demand for credit from the capital market. It is this effect that shows up in our steady state results. Bankruptcy cannot really occur in the above model but rather if there is a too strong credit expansion, the value of the firm will decline and with this the demand for credit declines. In fact the above model, as shown in Asada and Semmler (1995), may give rise to cyclical fluctuations rather than to bankruptcies of firms. As concerns the value of the firm, represented by the last column of Table 3.2, there is not always a monotonic change of the value of the firm as parameters change since those parameters affect through their new equilibrium values, g^* and d^*, and the asset price of the firm. Overall, the model portrays in a setup of a micro-macro link the interaction of credit market, credit financed investment, credit risk, the asset price of the firm and level of economic activity.

3.7 Conclusions

This chapter has employed perfect and imperfect capital market theory and discussed the relation of credit market borrowing, credit risk, asset prices and economic activity. We also have shown how in a simple model of the firm the micro-macro link may work. In the next chapter we want to pursue the question of how to empirically test for credit risk of economic agents and its impact on economic activity.

Chapter 4
Empirical Tests on Credit Market and Economic Activity

4.1 Introduction

In this chapter some key ideas on financial risk and economic activity will be tested. We are still mainly considering the credit market. If the lender faces credit risk, a risk of not recovering the loan from the borrower, this is because the borrower faces bankruptcy risk. Most modern financial analyses of financial risk in credit market use balance sheet variables of economic agents (households, firms, governments and countries) to derive some empirical measures for risk. In Sect. 4.2 we study the bankruptcy risk arising when firms borrow from capital markets to finance their activity. We will summarize some linear regression results. In Sect. 4.3. we introduce a nonlinear test of credit risk and economic activity using an econometric threshold model. In Sect. 4.4 we empirically study credit and bankruptcy risk when the intertemporal budget constraint is not fulfilled. The latter is undertaken in the context of a nonlinear intertemporal model.

4.2 Bankruptcy Risk and Economic Activity

4.2.1 Introduction: Measurement Problems

Here we will study the problem of financial risk from the point of view of the borrower. In our case the firms are borrowing from the capital market for investments. Indeed, since firms' investments are to a considerable extent financed through the credit market, this market may have a forceful impact on economic activity of firms and thus on the performance of the macroeconomy. We use balance sheet variables of firms to study the impact of bankruptcy risk on economic activity. Most of the studies are undertaken with OLS regressions. Such regression studies are, at least in a first approximation, helpful in uncovering the relation of bankruptcy risk and economic activity.

The role of balance sheet variables to measure financial risk is essential in the above theory of imperfect capital markets. As discussed above, when invoking the theory of asymmetric information, it is assumed that lenders and borrowers of funds have different knowledge about the possible success of the investment project. Given this information structure, lenders of funds will be unable to screen borrowers perfectly. Low-quality firms, when competing with high-quality firms for funds, have to pay a premium to obtain external funds. If overall bankruptcy risks or the spread between high- and low-quality firms increases in a downswing, agency and borrowing costs of external funds rise and this exerts a negative impact on investment. Net worth of low-quality firms is predicted to move pro-cyclically and borrowing costs of external funds counter cyclically, amplifying real economic disturbances.

The role of balance sheet variables to measure bankruptcy risk can also be found in Keynesian tradition, for example in the work of Minsky (1975, 1982, 1986) and, in particular, in the work of a contemporary of Keynes, namely Kalecki (1937a). Many scholars refer to him as an important source when studying the impact of the credit market and real activities. In Kalecki, particular emphasis is given to the risk that firms might find themselves exposed to when their activities are debt financed. Kalecki (1937a,b) referred to the role of real returns on investment, the interest rate, 'increasing risk' due to debt finance and a prospective rate of return as a determinant of investment. He then posited that the difference between the prospective and actual rate of return on capital is a measure of the risk incurred in the investment project. The cost of capital funds consists of the (real) interest rate and the cost of risk stemming from borrowing outside funds. The latter is considered to be an increasing function of the ratio at which investment is debt financed.[1] Thus, given default risk and a real interest rate, investment should vary with the expected rate of return or, for a given expected rate of return and real interest rate, investment is expected to vary (inversely) with the risk arising from the investment decisions. In any case the theory of imperfect capital markets presented in Chap. 3 as well as the Keynesian–Kaleckian tradition suggest a strong role for balance sheet variables in the activity of firms.[2] Yet, measuring bankruptcy risk of firms by using balance sheets, is not an unambiguous task. Moreover, testing for the influence of risk variables on firms' investment requires also to simultaneously control for other forces impacting investment.

To account for real forces affecting investment, often the accelerator principle, or some variant of it, has been employed. As the real variable we will use capacity utilization. This reflects the real accelerator and has traditionally been used in investment studies.[3] There are strong co-movements between the utilization of capacity and the actual rate of return on investment. The utilization of capacity is also used as the basic reference variable against which the contributions of other variables are measured.

Next we might want to take into account the movements of the (real) interest rate. Although (some) macro theories point in the direction of a lesser importance of the

---

[1]Kalecki (1937a) argues that investment will be undertaken up to the point where the excess of prospective profits over the interest rate is equated to the bankruptcy risk arising from debt financing of the investment project. Therefore, the cost of funds consists of two components: the interest rate and the 'increasing risk' due to debt finance. References to Kalecki's work can also be found in the recent work on imperfect capital markets.

[2]The role of the financial variables for investment had partly been lost in the Keynesian literature in the post-war period.

[3]The subsequent study is based on Franke and Semmler (1997). This study also tests the impact of the real return on capital from firms' investment. The results are very similar to using the utilization of capacity.

interest rate for investment,[4] we nevertheless prefer not to exclude the real interest rate as an independent variable.

Traditionally, empirical studies of bankruptcy risk have employed variables such as credit flow, the debt-asset ratio and the interest coverage ratio[5] as appropriate proxies for the default risk of firms. Other studies have proposed liquidity variables as proxies for risk rather then debt variables. An important variable to measure the default risk of firms is interest rate spreads. Low-quality firms – financially fragile firms – face a higher bankruptcy risk because their net worth is lower, external financing costs are higher than for high-quality firms. Thus, it is the financial market evaluation of firms' default risk that leads to interest rate spreads. Therefore, interest rate spread might be a very appropriate measure for bankruptcy risk. One thus expects, for example, in a stage of declining economic activity, an increasing interest rate spread and in particular, an increasing spread between low- and high-quality bonds. If lenders can accurately assess the default risk of individual firms or industries, the changes of risk will be reflected in interest rate spreads. As an aggregate measure of the spread to be used as proxy for risk we take the difference between the short-term commercial paper rate and the interest rate of Treasury bonds.[6]

We also suggest to including M2 as an additional factor in investment decisions. Money and money expansion by the monetary authority will provide liquidity for firms and ease the tension of default risk. More specifically, we employ the velocity of M2 money among the independent variables. If there is a strong endogenous money supply via banks in the business cycle then one might expect a counter cyclical movement in M2 velocity. Yet, the money supply is also affected by monetary policy. If a restrictive monetary policy is pursued during the late period of a boom, for example, and continued at the beginning of recessionary periods, this might contribute to a counter cyclical movement in M2 velocity, a liquidity crunch and thus to a (possibly lagged) decline in investment.

A more difficult problem is to measure prospective profits. If the stock market was a good predictor for firms' prospective profits one could rely on Tobin's Q as an important factor in investment decisions of firms. We do include Tobin's Q among the independent variables. On the other hand, one might argue that investment decisions depend more directly on business prospects. This suggests that we employ variables such as, for example, the leading indicators for estimating firms' expected return. In the subsequent part we therefore add to the independent variables an aggregate form of the leading indicators. Also the arithmetic average of Tobin's Q and that aggregate measure is invoked.[7]

---

[4] See Greenwald and Stiglitz (1986).

[5] The debt-asset ratio and interest coverage ratio may be considered as important variables in Minsky type models.

[6] Friedman and Kuttner (1992) have already employed interest rate spreads as measures for financial fragility. There, however, other proxies for financial risk are left aside. Interest rate spread has also been proposed as an additional leading indicator by Stock and Watson (1989).

[7] We want to point out here that Keynes, for example, never thought of a variable solely reflecting the financial evaluation of the firm, as being the most important determinant of investment. He more accurately referred to the 'state of confidence of investors' and business prospects when

We can now summarize the empirical measures that are employed in the following regressions. We study only a limited time period and use US quarterly data for the period 1960.4–1982.4. Because of some non-stationarity the data is detrended. The trend deviations of the growth rate of capital stock is taken as the dependent variable. The variable is gkDev. The capital stock data are from Fair (1984). As interest rate variable we take the 6 months commercial paper rate, deflated by the growth rate of GDP deflator. It is called irealDev. Both are from Citibase (1989). As financial variables, from the balance sheets of firms, in a preliminary step we have explored credit market debt (stock variable), gscmdDev, liquid assets, liquDev, quick assets and a measure for working capital.[8] Because of insignificance in the regressions (or the high collinearity with the other variables) we have dropped the quick ratio and the working capital variables from our financial regressions. Moreover, we take as interest coverage ratio icovDev. For the M2 money stock variable we take the M2-velocity of money which is called velocDev. All other variables are used as ratios over capital stock and then detrended by a segmented trend. Therefore, Dev stands for deviation. Data are from Citibase (1989). As said above, the interest rate spread is measured by the difference between the six months commercial paper rate and the six months Treasury bill rate (Citibase Data 1989), called sprdDev. Tobin's Q, called qsumDev, and an aggregate of the leading indicator, called deleadDev, as well as a linear combination (with equal weights) of qsumDev and dleadDev, called confDev, are added (as different variables) to measure expected returns.[9]

4.2.2 Some Empirical Results

The following Table 4.1 summarizes the regression results for our test of the impact of financial risk on firms' investment. Here we exclude interest rate spread, sprdDev.

As observable from the table the real variable, nDev, has the strongest and always significant impact on firm investment. The impact of the real interest rate is mostly insignificant. The influence of the financial risk variables are very fragile, sometimes significant, sometimes not, depending on what other variables are included. The profit expectations variable comes out mostly significant (except for qsumDev).[10]

---

discussing the role of expectations (Keynes, 1936, Chaps. 5 and 12). This includes general business conditions, consumption behavior, credit conditions and financial market prospects. It is on these grounds that we will refer to financial as well as to business prospects of firms in our regressions.

[8]The above measures were used in real terms (in 1982 dollars) with the following definitions: (1) flow and stock of credit market debt = net flows of corporate debt instruments; (2) liquid asset = stock of liquid assets; (3) working capital = stock of working capital; (4) interest coverage ratio = cash flows over net interest paid by non-financial cooperations (Fair, 1984). The data for these variables are taken from the Flow of Funds Accounts (1989).

[9]In order to construct an aggregate predictor for expected returns we aggregate with equal weights the four leading indicators of Business Conditions Digest (Citibase Data, 1989). The leading indicators are *dleac* (composite index, capital investment), *dlead* (composite index, inventory investment and purchase), *dleap* (composite index, profitability) and *dleaf* (composite index, money and financial flows).

[10]Note that the last column in this as well as the next table reports regression results that are corrected for auto-correlation.

Table 4.1. Test of the role of bankruptcy risk variables for investment, 1960:4 to 1982:4, (exclusive of interest rate spread variable) with gkDev as dependent variable

	1	2	3	4	5	6	7	8	9
$uDev_{-3}$	.305		.236	.243	.234	.261	.256	.248	.138
	(16.2)		(9.3)	(9.7)	(8.7)	(13.7)	(12.0)	(8.2)	(3.6)
$liquDev_{-1}$		.342	.087	.011				.049	
		(2.9)	(1.1)	(.2)				(.5)	
$velocDev_{-2}$		-.136	-.038	.009				-.032	
		(6.7)	(2.2)	(.5)				(1.6)	
$gscmdDev_{-1}$			.169	.122			.150	.028	.023
			(3.0)	(2.1)			(2.5)	(.5)	(.8)
$gscmdDev_{-2}$		.348							
		(4.7)							
$irealDev_{-2}$				-.025			-.053	-.034	-.006
				(.8)			(1.8)	(1.0)	(.3)
$ircovrDev_{-2}$				.004				-.0006	
				(2.2)				(.3)	
$qsumDev_{-2}$					.004				
					(.5)				
$dleadDev_{-2}$					.068				
					(4.1)				
$confDev_{-2}$						.035	.024	.031	.041
						(2.6)	(1.8)	(2.0)	(2.4)
ρ									.87
									(13.1)
R^2 adjusted	.76	.58	.79	.80	.79	.77	.79	.78	.89
S.E.	.58	.77	.54	.54	.54	.56	.54	.56	.38
DW	.62	.64	.78	.85	.60	.60	.80	.60	1.70

Next we want to show the regression results for the inclusion of the interest rate spread variable sprdDev.

As the results of Table 4.2 show the interest rate spread variable, sprdDev, is always significant and its influence on investment is strong, no matter what other variables are included in the regression.

4.2.3 Conclusions

It is hard to accurately measure the impact of bankruptcy risk on firm activity. The real variable, capacity utilization, is the most dominant variable explaining firm investment. Some bankruptcy risk variables are also significant, but they are often replaced

Table 4.2. Test of the role of bankruptcy risk for investment, 1960:4–1982:4 (inclusive of interest rate spread), with gkDev as dependent variable

	1	2	3	4	5	6	7	8	9
$uDev_{-1}$	.237		.253	.237	.253	.264	.246	.237	.152
	(16.2)		(11)	(9.3)	(11.0)	(14.4)	(12.8)	(9.2)	(4.4)
$liquDev_{-1}$		.275	-.003	-.027				-.025	
		(2.3)	(0.5)	(.35)				(3)	
$velocmDev_{-2}$		-.109	.007	.017				.018	
		(4.6)	(.4)	(.87)				(9)	
$gscmdDev_{-1}$			.147	.167			.140	.170	.041
			(2.9)	(3.2)			(2.7)	(2.9)	(1.4)
$gscmdDev_{-2}$		.347							
		(4.7)							
$irealDev_{-2}$				.006			.001	.007	.007
				(.22)			(.05)	(.2)	(.4)
$icvorDev_{-2}$				.002				-.003	
				(1.4)				(1.3)	
$sprdDev_{-3}$	-.118	-.079	-.115	-.114	-.100	-.110	-.110	-.110	-.070
	(5.8)	(2.1)	(4.8)	(4.5)	(3.8)	(5.1)	(4.8)	(4.5)	(3.6)
$gsumDev_{-2}$					.005				
					(.7)				
$dleadDev_{-2}$					.022				
					(1.2)				
$confDev_{-2}$						.015	.005	.002	0.30
						(1.3)	(.5)	(.2)	(1.8)
ρ									.83
									(11.6)
R^2 adjusted	.83	.60	.84	.84	.83	.82	.83	.83	.90
S.E.	.50	.76	.48	.48	.49	.49	.48	.48	.36
DW	.75	.73	.84	.85	.68	.72	.80	.86.	1.88

in their influence by other variables when they are included. In particular the interest rate spread variable is an important variable measuring bankruptcy risk and its impact on firm activity. We also want to note that this interest rate spread variable has also been proposed as an additional variable for a leading indicator by Stock and Watson (1989) who showed the relevance of this variable for indicating turning points of the business cycle. How well spread is measuring default risk is also discussed in Friedman and Kuttner (1992) and Bernanke and Blinder (1992) who point to the fact that the interest rate spread is also impacted by monetary policy. Kashyap, Stein and

Wilcox (1993) use another variable to measure credit market conditions and its input on economic activity. They use a variable for financial mix measured as L/(L+CP) whereby L represents loans from banks and CP the loans from the commercial paper markets. Finally, we want to note that we have undertaken our analysis on an aggregate level. This may wash out some stronger effects that might be visible on the firm level. Balance sheet variables on the firm level would have been more appropriate to measure bankruptcy risk and its impact on firm activity. Finally, we want to note that the low DW indicates some remaining structure in the residuals. This might suggest using nonlinear models for the impact of the credit market on economic activity. This will be taken up next.

4.3 Liquidity and Economic Activity in a Threshold Model

4.3.1 Introduction

Bankruptcy arises when an economic agent is unable to repay a loan. Whether or not there is a threat that the borrower cannot repay the loan can only be judged in an intertemporal context. Only in the long run, when the intertemporal budget constraint cannot be met will the agent run into bankruptcy. This is an aspect of debt contracts that will be studied empirically in Sect. 4.4. Yet, whenever the agent can obtain short term credit, i.e. if some creditor is willing to provide the agent with short term liquidity, the agent, at least temporarily can remain operative. What we consider next is under what conditions the agent might obtain liquidity. This problem of liquidity has been discussed in numerous economic studies.

From a micro perspective the credit market theory discussed in Chap. 3 is relevant to explain liquidity constraints for agents. As shown, if lenders are unable to perfectly monitor borrowers' investment projects, the balance sheets of agents and the agents' collateral is important for obtaining credit.[11] Households' and firms' net worth appears to move with the business cycle. In fact net worth moves pro cyclically. Then there will be less credit constraints for households and firms in high levels of economic activity compared to low levels of economic activity.

As has been shown in economic studies[12] most households, for example, are in fact liquidity constrained and cannot borrow against future income. This implies a close connection between income and spending.[13] Though available liquidity for those types of households – for example liquid assets such as deposits and treasury bonds – may be dissociated to some extent from income and spending, credit constraints would, however, effectively still play a major role in those households' spending behavior

---

[11]An increase in the marginal default risk is usually translated into higher cost of external compared to internal funds but we largely neglect here the cost of credit.

[12]See, for example, Campbell and Mankiw (1989) and Zeldes (1990).

[13]See Hubbard and Judd (1986) and also Deaton (1991). Both studies survey extensively the literature on excess sensitivity of spending with respect to income changes of liquidity constrained households. Deaton (1991), however, shows that, to some extent, this excess sensitivity is modified by precautionary savings of liquidity constrained households.

in that the ease and tightness of credit constraints over the business cycle would accelerate the contractions and expansions. This is in strong contrast to intertemporal models of consumer behavior which allow for intertemporal borrowing and lending. Here spending is dissociated from current income. Those types of consumers can use assets as collateral for borrowing and smooth out spending.

If, however, the majority of households are credit constrained this would support the hypothesis that spending is constrained by the ease and tightness of credit. A related argument can be made, see for example Fazzari et al. (1988), with respect to firms and their investment spending. Large firms that are evaluated on the stock market may not face credit constraints as much as small firms that are credit dependent. For small firms, mostly credit or bank dependent firms, the degree of credit constraints may vary over the business cycle – depending on the net worth or availability of credit for those firms. This, in turn, similar to liquidity constrained households, may act as a magnifying force for economic activity. Thus, overall, these observations for households and firms – as much as liquidity constraints are valid for households and a large number of small firms – predict that swings in households' and firms' balance sheet variables will magnify fluctuations in spending in the business cycle.[14]

Such an interaction of liquidity and output in the business cycle have been explored empirically in a large number of macroeconomic studies, for example in the papers by Eckstein, Green and Sinai (1974), Eckstein and Sinai (1986); and also Friedman (1986) and Blinder (1989). Modelling liquidity effects in the tradition of Keynesian theory have been undertaken within the context of IS-LM models.[15] Interesting non-linear versions of IS-LM[16] macro dynamics can be found in Day and Shafer (1985) and Day and Lin (1991). Those types of models exhibit quite intriguing periodic and non-periodic fluctuations in macro aggregates. In Foley (1987), besides money, commercial credit is introduced where firms are free to borrow and lend. Banks provide loans and offer deposits so that the overall source of liquidity is commercial credit and deposits. Here, too, strong fluctuations in aggregates can arise.

Thus, there is a long tradition that predicts empirically that credit may impact economic activity in a nonlinear way.[17] As aforementioned we here employ a simple version of a nonlinear macro dynamic model, developed by Semmler and Sieveking (1993), to give some predictions of the behavior of variables such as liquidity and output particularly over the business cycle. The model employed here which is testable by time series data allows for state-dependency and regime changes.

---

[14]We also want to note that liquidity and available credit may have smoothing effects on production or consumption at least for small shocks. Thus, actual economies may exhibit corridor-stability, see Semmler and Sieveking (1993). In this view small shocks do not give rise to deviation amplifying fluctuations but large shocks can lead to a different regime of propagation mechanism. Thus, only large shocks are predicted to result in magnified economic activities.

[15]Different variants of models on liquidity and output for a growing economy, are discussed in Flaschel, Franke and Semmler (1997), Chap. 4,

[16]See Semmler (1989).

[17]An excellent survey of earlier theories are given in Boyd and Blatt (1988). The work of Minsky (1978) continues this theoretical tradition.

Of course, as many economists have stressed, credit flows and liquidity also depend on monetary policy. The credit view of three transmission mechanisms of monetary policy maintains that it operates through the asset side of banks' balance sheets.[18] When reserves are reduced, and banks can only imperfectly substitute away from the reduced monetary base, then the volume of loans as well as the interest rates on loans and commercial papers are affected. Given the asymmetric information between borrowers and lenders, banks tend to become more careful in the selection of customers and this leads to an overall cutback in bank lending. Banks have to decrease the volume of loans, it is argued, they will extend loans only to the most secure customers or to customers with sound balance sheets and good collateral. Therefore, the ease and tightness of credit that firms and households face due to their own balance sheets and collaterals is easily seen to be accentuated by monetary policy. The importance of this credit channel for monetary policy has already been observed in earlier papers on the financial-real interaction. The papers by Eckstein et al. (1974, 1986) and Sinai (1992) are good examples. There it is shown that there are certain periods in the financial history of the US where monetary contractions have led to credit crunchs and a worsening of the above described borrowing situation for households and firms.[19] On the other hand monetary policy has helped to give rise, after a recessionary period, to a reliquification of households and firms and an improvement in their balance sheets.[20]

In empirical studies that employ time series analysis, however, it turns out to be rather difficult to give quantitative evaluation of the link between liquidity and economic activity.[21] There are complicated lead and lag patterns in the liquidity and output interaction and thus it is not easy to identify the liquidity-output link in the data, particularly if only linear regression models are employed.

There is, however, plenty of indirect empirical evidence that credit moves pro-cyclically[22] and that a nonlinear relation of liquidity and output is likely to be to be found in the data. The liquidity-output relation may be state dependent and undergo regime changes depending on the phases of the business cycle. A model that captured those nonlinear interactions is introduced in Semmler and Sieveking (1993) and econometrically studied in Koçkesen and Semmler (1997). Here, the liquidity and output interaction are state dependent in the sense that the relation of the variables change as some variables pass through certain thresholds. Recently, a number of

---

[18] For further details, see Chap. 10.

[19] The worsening of liquidity for firms and households with a restricted monetary policy is discussed in Sinai (1992).

[20] Sinai, for example, states: "Business upturns have almost always been associated with easier money and ample credit, lower interest rates... increased liquidity for households, business firms and financial institutions, (and) improved balance sheets..." (Sinai 1992:1)

[21] In earlier times the effects of monetary shocks were discussed in VAR type of money-output models with rather inconclusive results. A recent evaluation of the success and failure of those VAR studies is given in Bernanke and Blinder (1992).

[22] Pro-cyclical credit flows are documented in Friedman (1983), and Blinder (1989). Blinder, by decomposing credit market debt, finds that private credit market debt, in particular trade credit moves strongly pro-cyclically.

macro models have been proposed that exhibit state dependent reactions and regime changes with respect to the variables involved.[23]

A variety of eloborate univariate and multivariate statistical methods are capable of testing for state dependency and regime changes in time series data. Although there is no general agreement as to what type of nonlinear econometric model is best suited to modeling a given data series, important advances have been made. [24] Besides a direct test of state dependent reactions we can employ indirect methods such as the recently developed Smooth Transition Regression (STR) model that captures switching behavior and regime changes. The latter approach appears to be very useful to empirically study the dynamic interactions between variables. It has been applied with some success to the study of macroeconomic and financial time series. [25]

In our case, although the estimation strategy is not limited to this case, there are two variables to be examined as variables for state dependency and regime changes. Although there might be a choice of several important financial variables (that interact with real activity in a nonlinear fashion), we report results from a model that focuses on liquidity and output. These appear to us as the most relevant variables to test for the short-run nonlinear interaction of financial and real variables. We employ post-war US data.

4.3.2 A Simple Model

One can think of a nonlinear economic model on liquidity and economic activity as follows. Firms, households and banks may be represented by their balance sheets with assets on the left and liabilities on the right side. When the asset side, due to declining income flows, deteriorates, credit is harder to obtain and interest costs for the agents may rise. A rising interest rate may lead to an adverse selection problem and banks constrain or recall credit. Credit or credit lines represent liquidity for firms and households. So we will speak about liquidity as a general term representing (short term) credit. The following generic continuous time model, which is derived from an IS-LM model, see Koçkesen and Semmler (1997), may reveal our ideas:

$$\dot{\lambda} = \lambda f_1(\lambda, y) \tag{4.1}$$

$$\dot{y} = y f_2(\lambda, y) \tag{4.2}$$

---

[23] State dependent and threshold behavior of variables in economic and econometric models are frequently arising due to (non-convex) lumpy adjustment costs. Typical examples are the inventory, money holding and price adjustment models (Blanchard and Fischer 1989, Chap. 8), employment models with lumpy adjustment costs, but also monetary policy rules which are applied discretionarity after some variables have passed through their thresholds. The same may hold for employment policies of firms, for example, with firms adjusting to large deviations proportionally more than to small ones. For surveys of macroeconomic models of threshold type, see Flaschel, Franke and Semmler (1997).

[24] In the work by Tong (1990) a survey is given on many univariate models and Granger and Teräsvirta (1993) consider univariate as well as multivariate methods.

[25] For a survey and applications see Tong (1990), Granger and Teräsvirta (1993) and Granger, Teräsvirta and Anderson (1993), Ozaki (1986, 1987, 1994) and Rothman (1999).

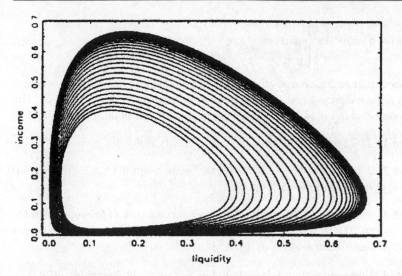

Fig. 4.1. Phase portrait

where $\lambda = L/K$, $y = Y/K$, with L denoting liquidity, y income and K the capital stock. We assume that, at least beyond a certain corridor about the steady state of the system (4.1)–(4.2), income and liquidity in Eq. (4.1) positively affects liquidity and also positively impacts income in Eq. (4.2).

The nonlinear relation of liquidity and economic activity means that the reactions of agents are amplitude dependent in that the spending of agents depends on the ease and tightness of credit. For liquidity constrained agents credit depends on net worth which moves pro-cyclically with risk falling in an economic boom and rising in a recession. Our model thus posits that spending accelerates (decelerates) when income and liquidity rises above (falls below) some threshold values. The same holds for liquidity. This dynamic is depicted in Fig. 4.1. Note that, of course, also credit cost – which depends on default risk; i.e. the wedge between cost of internal and external funds – moves counter cyclically.

The amplitude-dependent reactions can be made more explicit in the following specification

$$\dot{\lambda} = \lambda\left(\alpha - \beta y - \in_1 \lambda + g_1(\lambda, y)\right) \tag{4.3}$$

$$\dot{y} = y\left(-\gamma + \delta\lambda - \in_2 y + g_2(\lambda, y)\right) \tag{4.4}$$

where the g_i, with i=1,2 activate a regime change

$$g_i = g_i(\lambda, y) > 0 \text{ for } \begin{cases} \lambda > \mu_1 \quad \mu_1 > \lambda^* \\ \text{and} \\ y > \nu_1 \quad \nu_1 > y^* \end{cases}$$

$$g_i = g_i(\lambda, y) < 0 \text{ for } \begin{cases} \lambda < \mu_2 \quad \mu_2 < \lambda^* \\ \text{and} \\ y < \nu_2 \quad \nu_2 < y^* \end{cases}$$

In the upper regime there is a positive impact of liquidity and (or) spending whereas in the lower regime there is a negative perturbation of liquidity and (or) spending. The dynamic is depicted in Fig. 4.1. The following propositions can be shown to hold.

Proposition 1. *The System (4.3), (4.4) is asymptotically stable for $g_i = 0$*

Proposition 2. *If in system (4.3), (4.4) the perturbation terms $g_1(\lambda, y), g_2(\lambda, y) \neq 0$ are small enough it is asymptotically stable.*

Proposition 3. *For any $g_1(\lambda, y), g_2(\lambda, y) \neq 0$ system (4.3), (4.4) becomes unstable for $\in_1 = 0, \in_2 = 0$. The trajectories, however, remain in a positively invariant set for any $\in_1, \in_2 > 0$ even for large $g_1(\lambda, y), g_2(\lambda, y)$.*

A proof of these propositions can be found in Semmler and Sieveking (1993).

There is an extensive literature that estimates such state dependent models. An important contribution has been made by Ozaki (1985) who estimates for example a van der Pol equation written in continuous time

$$\ddot{x} - b(x)\dot{x} + bx = \varepsilon$$
$$\varepsilon \;:\; \text{white noise}$$
$$b(x) \;:\; a(1 - x^2).$$

A discrete time nonlinear model approximation of such a continuous time locally self exciting and globally bounded system is

$$x_t = (\emptyset_1 + \Pi_1 e^{-x_{t-1}^2})x_{t-1} + (\emptyset_2 + \Pi_2 e^{-x_{t-1}^2})x_{t-2} + \varepsilon_t.$$

A further example of a system with threshold behavior is a piecewise linear model such as

$$\begin{aligned} x_t &= \Pi(T_1)x_{t-1} + \varepsilon_t & \text{for } x_{t-1} < T_1 \\ &= \Pi(x_{t-1})x_{t-1} + \varepsilon_t & \text{for } T_1 \le x_{t-1} < T_2 \\ &= \Pi(T_2)x_{t-1} + \varepsilon_t & \text{for } x_{t-1} \ge T_2. \end{aligned}$$

Models that are written in continuous time

$$\dot{z} = f(z, \theta, w)$$

with θ the parameter set and w a noise term, can be discretized, for example, by the Euler approximation. The Euler method is[26]

---

[26] A different procedure is the method of local linearization used in Ozaki's work. There applications can be found to the van der Pol equation and random vibration systems, see Ozaki (1986, 1994).

$$z_{t+h} = z_t + hf(z/\theta) + \varepsilon_t$$

Popular discrete time nonlinear models are Threshold Autoregressive (TAR) models. They use local approximations to a nonlinear system by linear regimes via thresholds. A univariate TAR model is, for example,

$$Y_t = \alpha_i^{(j)} + \sum_{i=1}^{p} \alpha_i^{(j)} Y_{t-i} + \varepsilon_t^{(j)},$$
$$if\ r_{j-1} \leq Y_{t-d} < r_j,\ j = 1, 2, \dots.k$$

k = number of different regimes, d = delay parameter, $\{r_j\}$ = threshold parameters.

A multivariate TAR model reads

$$Y_t = \alpha_0^{(j)} + \sum_{i=1}^{p} \beta_i^{(j)} X_{t-i} + \varepsilon_t^{(j)},$$
$$if\ r_{j-1} \leq X_{t-d} < r_j$$

A large number of applications to macroeconomic and financial data have been undertaken for theses types of models, for example to GNP, stock market returns and unemployment rates, see Potter (1993), Tong (1990), and Rothman (1999).
We report estimation results of the above nonlinear (threshold) model for liquidity and output dynamics with unconstrained lag structure. A linearity test is embedded in a nonlinear threshold model. Results of the linearity test are reported in Table 4.3.

Table 4.3. Linearity Tests

Equation	Variable	p	p^3	p^2	p^1
Liquidity	ρ_{t-6}	0.06	0.43	0.33	0.008
Rate of return	λ_{t-7}	0.001	0.005	0.31	0.01

where p, p^3, p^2, p^1 refer to the probability values of certain (nested) hypotheses. For example, the linearity hypothesis is rejected at a 6% level of significance for the liquidity equation when the transition variable is ρ_{t-6}.
Results of the threshold estimations are:

$$\lambda_t = \underset{(.0004)}{.0008} + \underset{(.06)}{.75}\lambda_{t-1} + \underset{(.09)}{.55}\lambda_{t-5} - \underset{(.05)}{.22}\rho_{t-5} + \underset{(.05)}{.18}\rho_{t-6}$$

$$+ \left(-\underset{(.14)}{.56}\lambda_{t-3} - \underset{(.07)}{.18}\rho_{t-4} + \underset{(.12)}{.36}\rho_{t-5} - \underset{(.10)}{.39}\rho_{t-6} \right)$$

$$\times \left(1 + \exp\left[-\underset{(1.42)}{2.85} \times 72.59 \left(\rho_{t-6} - \underset{(.003)}{.005} \right) \right] \right)^{-1}$$

$$R^2 = 0.85 \qquad SE = 0.0029 \quad LM(7) = 1.81 \ (0.09)$$
$$ARCH(1) = 0.06 \ (0.81) \ BJ = 1.45 \ (0.48)$$

The LSTR model for rate of return is given by

$$\rho_t = \underset{(.001)}{.004} + \underset{(.14)}{.76}\lambda_{t-1} - \underset{(.20)}{.58}\lambda_{t-5} + \underset{(.06)}{.63}\rho_{t-1} - \underset{(.11)}{.34}\rho_{t-5} + \underset{(.11)}{.36}\rho_{t-6} - \underset{(.06)}{.21}\rho_{t-8}$$

$$+ \Bigg(\underset{(.003)}{.006} - \underset{(.27)}{1.02}\lambda_{t-4} + \underset{(.38)}{1.18}\lambda_{t-5}$$

$$- \underset{(.39)}{.82}\lambda_{t-7} + \underset{(.26)}{1.10}\lambda_{t-8} + \underset{(.18)}{.57}\rho_{t-5} - \underset{(.19)}{.53}\rho_{t-6} \Bigg)$$

$$\times \left(1 + \exp\left[\underset{(20.38)}{18.81} \times 138.50 \left(\lambda_{t-7} - \underset{(.0004)}{.0002} \right) \right] \right)^{-1}$$

$$R^2 = 0.79 \qquad SE = 0.007 \qquad LM(9) = 0.93 \ (0.51)$$
$$ARCH(1) = 7.17 \ (0.01) \ BJ = 0.093 \ (0.95) \ LIN(\rho_{t-8}) = 2.26 (0.01)$$

The results of the estimations are shown in Fig. 4.2

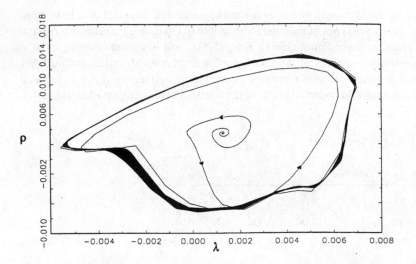

Fig. 4.2. Dynamics from a threshold model

As can be observed simulating the model with the estimated parameter values gives us the above shown figure. Details of the results are discussed in Koçkesen and Semmler (1998).

4.3.3 Conclusions

Threshold models are very suitable to model nonlinear relationships between economic variables. The threshold methodology has found application in numerous other fields in economics, see the contributions in Rothman (1999), see also Granger and

Teräsvirta (1993). We have shown that there is convincing evidence for nonlinearities in the financial and real interaction, in particular, as studied in the interaction of liquidity and output. Thus nonlinearity might be especially relevant for the relationship of liquidity and output since short term credit is usually tightly connected to agents' balance sheet variables, e.g. short- and long-term debt, leverage and physical capital or liquid assets as collateral. All of them move with the level of economic activity and economic activity in turn is significantly impacted by credit conditions. There are likely to be thresholds that play a role in this interaction. Yet, from the long term perspective agents are usually screened by the lenders or credit agencies whether their intertemporal budget constraint is fulfilled. We now turn to the problem of how one can evaluate whether the agent's intertemporal budget constraint is not violated.

4.4 Estimations of Credit Risk and Sustainable Debt

4.4.1 Introduction

As aforementioned sustainable debt has to be discussed in an intertemporal context. Economic agents (households, firms, governments and countries) are creditworthy as long as the present value of their income does not fall short of the liabilities that the agents face. Credit rating firms evaluate permanently the creditworthiness of creditors.[27] Debt sustainability and creditworthiness was at the root of the Asian financial crisis. A credit crisis can in fact trigger a financial crisis and large output losses. [28]

In this section we want to study and evaluate credit risk in the context of a dynamic economic model and propose an empirical test. More specifically we want to study borrowing capacity, creditworthiness and credit risk in the context of an economic growth model. In order to simplify matters we do not employ a stochastic version of a dynamic model but rather employ a deterministic framework.[29] Yet, our study might still be important for the issues of credit risk and management that have kept the attention of the financial economists since the Asian financial crisis.

Here we do not extensively discuss the diverse empirical variables and methods to evaluate credit risk and to compute default risk of bonds (see Benninga 1998, Chap. 17). Those methods are very useful in practice but have only little connection to a theory of credit risk and theoretical measures of creditworthiness. Measuring credit risk is also important in risk management and the value at risk approach. The latter approach works with expected volatility of asset prices (for a survey, see Duffie and Pan 1997). Although our study has implications for credit risk analysis in empirical finance literature and risk management our approach is more specifically related to the literature that links credit market and economic activity in the context of intertemporal models. In recent times this link has been explored in numerous papers that take an intertemporal perspective.

---

[27] For a detailed description of credit rating practices, see Benninga (1998), Chap. 17.

[28] See the work by Milesi-Ferreti and Razin (1996)

[29] A stochastic version can be found in Sieveking and Semmler (1999).

In one type of paper, mostly assuming perfect credit markets, it is assumed that, roughly speaking, agents can borrow against future income as long as the discounted future income, the wealth of the agents, is no smaller than the debt that agents have incurred. In this case there is no credit risk whenever the non-explosiveness condition holds. Positing that the agents can borrow against future income, the non-explosiveness condition is equivalent to the requirement that the intertemporal budget constraint holds for the agents. Formally, the necessary conditions for optimality, derived from the Hamiltonian equation, are often employed to derive the dynamics of the state variables and the so called transversality condition is used to provide a statement on the non-explosiveness of the debt of the economic agents. Models of this type have been discussed in the literature for households, firms, governments and small open economies (with access to international capital markets).[30]

In a second type of paper, and also often in practice, assuming credit market imperfections, economists presume that borrowing is constrained. Frequently, borrowing ceilings are assumed which are supposed to prevent agents from borrowing an unlimited amount. Presuming that the agents' assets serve as collateral, a convenient way to define the debt ceiling is to then assume the debt ceiling to be a fraction of the agents' wealth. The definition of debt ceilings have become standard, for example, in a Ramsey model of the firm, see Brock and Dechert (1985) or in a Ramsey growth model for small open economies; see, for example, Barro, Mankiw and Sala-i-Martin (1995). It has also been pointed out that banks often define debt ceilings for their borrowers, see Bhandari, Haque and Turnovsky (1990).

A third type of literature also assumes credit market imperfections but employs endogenous borrowing costs such as in the work by Bernanke and Gertler (1989, 1994) and further extensions to heterogenous firms, such as small and large firms, in Gertler and Gilchrist (1994). State dependent borrowing costs have been associated with the financial accelerator theory. Here one presupposes only a one period zero horizon model and then shows that due to an endogenous change of a firm's net worth, as collateral for borrowing, credit cost is endogenous. For potential borrowers their credit cost is inversely related to their net worth. In parallel other literature has posited that borrowers may face a risk dependent interest rate which is assumed to be composed of a market interest rate (for example, an international interest rate) and an idiosyncratic component determined by the individual degree of risk of the borrower. Various forms of the agent specific risk premium can be assumed. Here, it is often posited to be endogenous in the sense that it is convex in the agent's debt.[31]

Recent extensions of the third type of work have been undertaken by embedding credit market imperfections and endogenous borrowing cost more formally in intertemporal models such as the standard stochastic growth model, see Carlstrom and Fuerst (1997) and Bernanke, Gertler and Gilchrist (1998). Some of this literature has also dealt with the borrowing constraints of heterogenous agents (households,

---

[30]For a brief survey of such models for households, firms and governments or countries, see Blanchard and Fischer (1989, Chap. 2) and Turnovsky (1995).

[31]The interest rate as function of the default risk of the borrower is posited by Bhandari, Haque and Turnovsky (1990) and Turnovsky (1995).

firms) in an intertemporal general equilibrium framework. Although in this section we stress intertemporal behavior of economic agents, we will not deal with the case of heterogenous agents here.

We present a dynamic model with credit markets and asset prices that can be perceived as holding (true) for single agents or a country. In fact the set up of the model is undertaken in a way that reflects a country borrowing from abroad. Empirically we estimate instead the sustainability of foreign debt or assets of Euro-area countries where we readily have sufficient time series data available.

4.4.2 The Dynamic Model

First we give a formal presentation of the model that we want to estimate. In a contract between a creditor and debtor there are two problems involved. The first pertains to the computation of debt and the second to the computation of the debt ceiling. The first problem is usually answered by employing an equation of the form

$$\dot{B}(t) = \theta B(t) - f(t), \qquad B(0) = B_0$$

where $B(t)$ is the level of debt[32] at time t, θ the interest rate determining the credit cost and $f(t)$ the net income of the agent. The second problem can be settled by defining a debt ceiling such as

$$B(t) \leq C, \qquad (t > 0)$$

or less restrictively by

$$\sup_{t \geq 0} B(t) < \infty$$

or even less restrictively by the aforementioned transversality condition

$$\lim_{t \to \infty} e^{-\theta t} B(t) = 0. \tag{4.5}$$

The ability of a debtor to service the debt, i.e. the feasibility of a contract, will depend on the debtors source of income. Along the lines of intertemporal models of borrowing and lending[33] we model this source of income as arising from a stock of capital $k(t)$, at time t, which changes with THE investment rate $j(t)$ at time t through

$$\dot{k}(t) = j(t) - \sigma(k(t)), \quad k(0) = k_0. \tag{4.6}$$

In our general model both the capital stock and the investment are allowed to be multivariate. As debt service we take the net income from the investment rate $j(t)$ at

---

[32]Note that all subsequent state variables are written in terms of efficiency labor along the line of Blanchard (1983).

[33]Prototype models used as basis for our further presentation can be found in Blanchard (1983), Blanchard and Fischer (1989) or Turnovsky (1995).

capital stock level $k(t)$ minus some minimal rate of consumption.[34] Hence

$$\dot{B}(t) = \theta B(t)) - f\left(k(t), j(t)\right), \ B(0) = B_0 \tag{4.7}$$

where $\theta B(t)$ is the credit cost. Note that the credit cost is not necessarily a constant factor (a constant interest rate). We call $B^*(k)$ the creditworthiness of the capital stock k. The problem to be solved is how to compute B^*.

If there is a constant credit cost factor (interest rate), $\theta = \frac{H(B,k)}{B}$, then, it is easy to see, $B^*(k)$ is the present value of k or the asset price of k:

$$B^*(k) = \underset{j}{Max} \int_0^\infty e^{-\theta t} f\left(k(t), j(t)\right) dt - B(0) \tag{4.8}$$

s.t.

$$\dot{k}(t) = j(t) - \sigma\left(k(t)\right), \quad k(0) = k_0 \tag{4.9}$$

$$\dot{B}(t) = \theta B(t) - f\left(k(t), j(t)\right), \quad B(0) = B_0. \tag{4.10}$$

The more general case is, however, that θ is not a constant. As in the theory of credit market imperfections we generically may let θ depend on k and B.[35] Employing a growth model in terms of efficiency labor[36] we can use the following net income function that takes account of adjustment investment and adjustment cost of capital.

$$f(k, j) = k^\alpha - j - j^\beta k^{-\gamma} \tag{4.11}$$

where $\sigma > 0, \alpha > 0, \gamma > 0$ are constants.[37] In the above model $\sigma > 0$ captures both a constant growth rate of productivity as well as a capital depreciation rate and population growth.[38] Blanchard (1983) used $\beta = 2$, $\gamma = 1$ to analyze the optimal indebtedness of a country (see also Blanchard and Fischer 1989, Chap. 2).

Note that in the model (4.8)–(4.10) we have not used utility theory. However, as shown in Sieveking and Semmler (1998) the model (4.8)–(4.10) exhibits a strict relationship to a growth model built on a utility function, for example, such as[39]

---

[34]In the subsequent analysis of creditworthiness we can set consumption equal to zero. Any positive consumption will move down the creditworthiness curve. Note also that public debt for which the Ricardian equivalence theorem holds, i.e. where debt is serviced by a non-distortionary tax, would cause the creditworthiness curve to shift down. In computing the "present value" of the future net surpluses we do not have to assume a particular interest rate. Yet, in the following study we neither elaborate on the problem of the price level nor on the exchange rate and its effect on net debt and creditworthiness.

[35]The more general theory of creditworthiness with state dependent credit cost is provided in Grüne, Semmler and Sieveking (2002). Note that instead of relating the credit cost inversely to net worth, as in Bernanke, Gertler and Gilchrist (1998), one could use the two arguments, k and B, explicitly.

[36]The subsequent growth model can be viewed as a standard RBC model where the stochastic process for technology shocks is shut down and technical change is exogenously occurring at a constant rate.

[37]Note that the production function k^α may have to be multiplied by a scaling factor. For the analytics we leave it aside here.

[38]For details, see Blanchard (1983).

[39]For details, see Blanchard (1983).

$$Max \quad \int_0^\infty e^{-\theta t} u\left(c(t), k(t)\right) dt \tag{4.12}$$

s.t.

$$\dot{k}(t) = j(t) - \sigma\left(k(t)\right), \qquad k(0) = k. \tag{4.13}$$

$$\dot{B}(t) = \theta B(t) - f\left(k(t), j\right) + c(t), \qquad B(0) = B \tag{4.14}$$

with the transversality condition

$$\lim_{t \to \infty} e^{-\theta t} B(t) = 0 \tag{4.15}$$

which often turns up in the literature[40] among the "necessary conditions" for a solution of a welfare problem such as (4.12)–(4.15). In Sieveking and Semmler (1998) it is shown that the problem (4.12)–(4.15) can be separated into two problems. The first problem is to find optimal solutions that generate the present value of net income flows and the second problem is to study the path of how the present value of net income flows are consumed. There also, conditions are discussed under which such separation is feasible. The separation into those two problems appears to be feasible as long as the evolution of debt does not appear in the objective function. If such separation is feasible we then only need to be concerned with the model (4.8)–(4.10). Yet instead of maximizing a utility function, the present value of a net income function is maximized.

The maximization problem (4.8)–(4.10) can be solved by using the necessary conditions of the Hamiltonian for (4.8)–(4.9). Thus we maximize

$$\underset{j}{Max} \int_0^\infty e^{-\theta t} f(k(t), j(t)) dt$$

s.t. (4.9).

The Hamiltonian for this problem is

$$H(k, x, j, \lambda) = \max_j H(k, x, j, \lambda)$$

$$H(k, x, j, \lambda) = \lambda f(k, j) + x(j - \sigma k)$$

$$\dot{x} = \frac{-\partial H}{\partial k} + \theta x = (\sigma + \theta) x - \lambda f_k(k, j).$$

We denote x as the co-state variable in the Hamiltonian equations and λ is equal to 1.[41] The function $f(k, j.)$ is strictly concave by assumption. Therefore, there is a function $j(k, x)$ which satisfies the first order condition of the Hamiltonian

---

[40]See, for example, Bhandari, Hague and Turnovsky (1990). In our framework the equivalent transversality condition will be

$$\sup_{t \geq 0} B(t) < \infty$$

[41]For details of the computation of the equilibria in the case when one can apply the Hamiltonian, see Semmler and Sieveking (1998), appendix.

$$f_j(k, j) + x = 0 \tag{4.16}$$

$$j = j(k, x) = \left(\frac{x - 1}{k^{-\gamma} \cdot \beta}\right)^{\frac{1}{\beta - 1}} \tag{4.17}$$

and j is uniquely determined thereby. It follows that (k, x) satisfy

$$\dot{k} = j(k, x) - \sigma k \tag{4.18}$$

$$\dot{x} = (\sigma + \theta)x - f_k(k, j(k, x)) \tag{4.19}$$

The isoclines can be obtained by the points in the (k, x) space for $\beta = 2$ where $\dot{k} = 0$ satisfies

$$x = 1 + 2\sigma k^{1-\gamma} \tag{4.20}$$

and where $\dot{x} = 0$ satisfies

$$x_{\pm} = 1 + \vartheta k^{1-\gamma} \pm \sqrt{\vartheta^2 k^{2-2\gamma} + 2\vartheta k^{1-\gamma} - 4\alpha\gamma^{-1}k^{\alpha-\gamma}} \tag{4.21}$$

where $\vartheta = 2\gamma^{-1}(\sigma + \theta)$. Note that the latter isocline has two branches.

If the parameters are given, the steady state – or steady states, if there are multiple ones – can be computed and then the local and global dynamics studied. We scale the production function by α [42] and take $c = 0$. We employ the following parameters: $\alpha = 1.1, \gamma = 0.3, \sigma = 0.15, \theta = 0.1$.

For those parameters, using the Hamiltonian approach, there are two positive candidates for equilibria. The two equilibrium candidates are: (HE1): $k^* = 1.057$, $x^* = 1.3$ and (HE2): $k^{**} = 0.21, x^{**} = 1.1$. A third equilibrium candidate is $k = 0$. [43]

4.4.3 Estimating the Parameters

Next, we want to take our growth model with adjustment costs of investment to the data. It would be interesting to pursue this with time series data for Asian countries before the financial crisis 1997–98. Yet, there are no reliable long-term data sets available. We will thus use quarterly data from Euro-area countries. We could generate time series data for the relevant variables for most of the core countries of the Euro-area. For the purpose of parameter estimation we have to transform our dynamic equations into estimable equations. By presuming the version, where only a constant credit factor enters the debt equation, we can employ the Hamiltonian equation. This is justified in the case of Euro-area countries, since there are likely to be no severe idiosyncratic risk components in the interest rate. We can transform the system into estimable equations and employ time series data on capital stock and investment – all expressed in efficiency units – to estimate the involved parameter set.

---

[42] We have multiplied the production function by $a = 0.30$ in order to obtain sufficiently separated equilibria.

[43] We want to stress again that from the Hamiltonian equation one can only obtain candidates for equilibria.

Substituting the optimal investment rate (4.17) into (4.18) we get the following two dynamic equations

$$\dot{k} = \left(\frac{x-1}{k^{-\gamma}\cdot\beta}\right)^{\frac{1}{\beta-1}} - \sigma k \tag{4.22}$$

$$\dot{x} = (\sigma + \theta)x - \alpha k^{\alpha-1} - j^{\beta}\gamma k^{(-\gamma-1)}. \tag{4.23}$$

Next, we transform the above system into observable variables so that we obtain estimable dynamic equations.

From (4.22) we obtain

$$\hat{k} = j/k - \sigma \tag{4.24}$$

with $\hat{k} = \dot{k}/k$. Note that from the determination of j in (4.22) we can get

$$x = 1 + \beta j^{\beta-1}k^{-\gamma}. \tag{4.25}$$

Taking the time derivative we obtain

$$\dot{x} = \left(\beta(\beta-1)j^{\beta-2}k^{-\gamma}\right)\cdot\dot{j} \tag{4.26}$$

and using (4.23) we have

$$\left(\beta(\beta-1)j^{\beta-2}k^{-\gamma}\right)\cdot\dot{j} = (\sigma+\theta)x - \alpha k^{\alpha-1} - j^{\beta}\gamma k^{(-\gamma-1)}.$$

Thus

$$\dot{j} = \frac{(\sigma+\theta)x - \alpha k^{\alpha-1} - j^{\beta}\gamma k^{(-\gamma-1)}}{\beta(\beta-1)j^{\beta-2}k^{-\gamma}} \tag{4.27}$$

or

$$\hat{j} = \frac{\dot{j}}{j} = \left(\frac{(\sigma+\theta)x - \alpha k^{\alpha-1} - j^{\beta}\gamma k^{(-\gamma-1)}}{\beta(\beta-1)j^{\beta-2}k^{-\gamma}}\right)/j \tag{4.28}$$

Substituting (4.25) into (4.27) we get as estimable equations in observable variables (4.24) and (4.28) which depend on the following parameter set to be estimated.

$$\varphi = (\theta, \sigma, \beta, \gamma, \alpha, a)$$

The estimation of the above parameter set is undertaken by aggregating capital stock and investment for the core countries of the Euro-area. The data are quarterly data from 1978.1–1996.2. Although aggregate capital stock data, starting from 1970.1 are available, we apply our estimation to the period 1978.1–1996.2. This is because the European Monetary System was introduced in 1978 whereby the exchange rates between the countries where fixed within a band. This makes the cross-country aggregation of capital stock and investment feasible. The aggregate capital stock series is gross private capital stock and the investment series is total fixed investment. Both are taken from the OECD data base (1999). The series for gross capital stock and investment represent aggregate real data for Germany, France, Italy, Spain, Austria, Netherlands and Belgium. Since we are employing a model on labor efficiency each country's time series for capital stock and investment is scaled down by labor in efficiency units measured by the time series $L_t = L_0 e^{(n+g_{y/l})t}$ where n is average population growth and $g_{y/l}$ average productivity growth. As to our estimation strategy we employ NLLS estimation and use a constrained optimization procedure.[44] The results are shown in Table 4.4.

Table 4.4. Parameter estimates for Euro-area countries (1978.1–1996.2)

θ	σ	β	γ	α	a
0.035	0.092	0.312	0.116	0.385	3.32

The parameters obtained from the historical data are quite reasonable.[45] Overall one can observe that the adjustment costs of investment are not very large since the exponents β and γ are small.

Using the estimated parameters one can again compute through (4.16)–(4.20) the steady states for the capital stock. Doing so numerically, it turns out that for our parameter estimates (table 4.4) the steady state is unique and we obtain a $k^* = 37.12$. This coincides, roughly, with the mean of the historical series of capital stock for Euro-area countries. This gives a steady state net income of $f(k, j) = 8.799$, computed from (4.11) at the steady state of $k^* = 37.12$. Moreover, for the present value of the net income at the steady state we obtain $V(k^*) = 244.4193$.

Using the estimated parameters Fig. 4.3 shows the computed output, investment (including adjustment costs of investment) and the net income. As Fig. 4.3 shows, since we are using aggregate variables in efficiency units, the output in efficiency units tends to be stationary and the net income moves inversely to investment (the latter including adjustment costs).

Finally, note that with those parameter estimates given in Table 4.4 we could now easily compute the present value outside the steady state and thus the critical debt curve by using the Hamilton-Jacobi-Bellman equation, see Grüne, Semmler and Sieveking (2002). Since, however, there is no external debt of Euro-area countries but rather external assets, as shown in the next section, the result of such an exercise will not be very instructive. The balance sheets of banks and firms, as discussed in Krugman (1999a,b) and Mishkin (1998), will presumably show no sign of deterioration, since the Euro-area countries have net claims vis-a-vis the rest of the world. Our methods of

---

[44]The estimations were undertaken in GAUSS for which the constrained optimization procedure recently provided by GAUSS was used.

[45]We want to note that standard errors could not be recovered since the Hessian in the estimation was not non-negative definite.

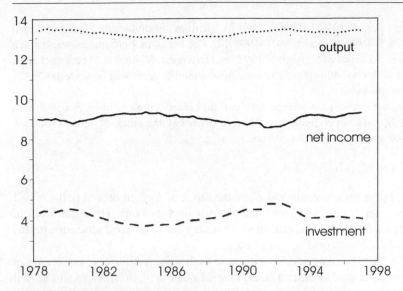

Fig. 4.3. Net income, investment and output

computing the present value of net income could, however, be fruitfully undertaken for other countries with deteriorating external debt and balance sheets of banks and firms.[46] Note, however, that the above method gives us only asymptotic results, i.e. if $t \to \infty$. Next, for Euro-area countries we pursue another method – for a finite number of observations – to compute the sustainability of external assets.

4.4.4 Testing Sustainability of Debt

Next, following Flood and Garber (1980) and Hamilton and Flavin (1986) a NLLS estimate for the sustainability of external debt can be designed for a finite number of observations. Similar to the computation of the capital stock and investment for our core countries of Euro-area countries we have computed the trade account, the current account and the net foreign assets of those core countries for the time period 1978.1–1998.1. Since we want to undertake sustainability tests for certain growth regimes, we have computed monthly observations. In our computation we had to eliminate the trade among the Euro-area countries.[47] We consider the time series

---

[46] Of course, one would have to consider also the exchange rate regime under which the country borrows and in particular the fact whether the country (banks, firms) borrows in foreign currency. In this case an exchange rate shock will exacerbate the deterioration of the balance sheets, see Mishkin (1998) and Krugman (1999 a,b).

[47] A similar attempt to compute external debt of countries and regions, following a similar methodology as suggested above, has been recently undertaken by Lane and Milesi-Ferreti (1999). Their results for the Euro-area core countries show similar trends as our computation. Their results are, however, less precise since they do not eliminate intra-Euro-area countries trade.

for the entire period 1978.1–1998.12 and in addition subdivide the period into two periods 1978.1–1993.12. and 1994.1–1998.12. The break in 1994 makes sense since the exchange rate crisis of September 1992 lead to a reestablishment of new exchange rates with a wider band in 1993. Thus, the sustainability tests will be undertaken for those two subperiods.

In a discrete version the foreign debt can be computed as follows. Starting with initial debt B_0 one can compute in a discrete time way the stock of debt as follows. By assuming a constant interest rate we have

$$B_t = (1 + r_{t-1})B_{t-1} - TA_t \qquad (4.29)$$

where TA_t is the trade account and B_{t-1} the stock of foreign debt at period $t - 1$ and r_{t-1} the interest rate. As interest rate we took the Libor rate. The initial stock of foreign debt B_0 for 1978.1 was estimated. This way, the entire time series of external debt and trade account could be generated.

From Eq. (4.29) we can develop a discrete time sustainability test. For reason of simplicity let us assume a constant interest rate. Equation (4.29) is then a simple first order difference equation that can be solved by recursive forward substitution leading to

$$B_t = \sum_{i=t+1}^{N} \frac{TA_i}{(1 + r)^{i-t}} + \frac{(1 + r)^t B_N}{(1 + r)^N}. \qquad (4.30)$$

In the Eq. (4.30) the second term must go to zero if the intertemporal budget constraint is supposed to hold. Then Eq. (4.30) means that the current value of debt is equal to the expected discounted future trade account surplus

$$B_t = E_t \sum_{i=t+1}^{\infty} \frac{TA_i}{(1 + r)^{i-t}}. \qquad (4.31)$$

Equivalent to requiring that Eq. (4.31) be fulfilled, is the following condition:

$$E_t \lim_{N \to \infty} \frac{B_N}{(1 + r)^N} = 0. \qquad (4.32)$$

The equation is the usual transversality condition or No-Ponzi game condition as discussed in Sect. 4.4.2.

If the external debt is constrained not to exceed a constant, A_0, on the right hand side of (4.30), we then have

$$B_t = E_t \sum_{i=t+1}^{\infty} \frac{TA_i}{(1 + r)^{i-t}} + A_0(1 + r)^t \qquad (4.33)$$

The NLLS test proposed by Flood and Garber (1980) and Hamilton and Flavin (1986) and Greiner and Semmler (1999) can be modified for our case. It reads:

$$TA_t = b_1 + b_2 TA_{t-1} + b_3 TA_{t-2} + b_4 TA_{t-3} + \varepsilon_{2t} \qquad (4.34)$$

$$B_t = b_5(1+r)^t + b_6 + \frac{(b_2 b + b_3 b^2 + b_4 b^3)TA_t}{(1 - b_2 b - b_3 b^2 - b_4 b^3)}$$

$$+\frac{(b_3 b + b_4 b^2)TA_{t-1}}{(1 - b_2 b - b_3 b^2 - b_4 b^3)} + \frac{(b_4 b)TA_{t-2}}{(1 - b_2 b - b_3 b^2 - b_4 b^3)} + \varepsilon_{1t} \qquad (4.35)$$

We want to note, however, that following Wilcox (1989) it might be reasonable to compute trade account surplus and debt series as discounted time series. We have also undertaken the computation of those discounted time series by discounting both the trade account and the external debt with an average interest rate and performed the above (4.34)–(4.35) sustainability test.

Figure 4.4 shows the undiscounted and discounted time series for external assets of the Euro-area.

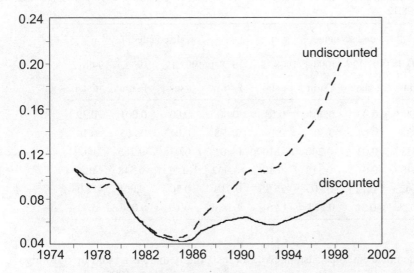

Fig. 4.4. Undiscounted and discounted net foreign assets

Table 4.5 reports test results for both types of time series for the entire time period 1978.1–1998.12.

Table 4.6 reports our estimation results for subperiods again for both undiscounted and discounted trade account and debt service. The results of estimation of the coefficients as to the relevance of non-sustainability of foreign assets for the Euro-area are not very conclusive. The coefficient b_5, which is the relevant coefficient in our context, has the correct sign but is always insignificant.

Next we compute the estimate (4.34)–(4.35) for the two subperiods. Table 4.6 reports the results for undiscounted and discounted variables respectively.

As can clearly be seen from the coefficient b_5 both the undiscounted and the discounted trade time series show a rapid built-up of net foreign assets of the Euro-

Table 4.5. Sustainability test of Euro debt, 1978.1–1998.12

	undiscounted		discounted	
Param	Estim	t-stat	Estim	t-stat
b_1	0.00	0.00	0.00	0.00
b_2	0.76	0.05	0.53	0.04
b_3	0.45	-0.02	0.37	0.02
b_4	-0.51	-0.05	-0.06	-0.07
b_5	-0.07	-1.20	-0.002	-0.04
b_6	0.0051	0.06	-0.064	-0.88

Table 4.6. Sustainability test of foreign debt for Euro-area countries, 1978.1–1993.12 and 1994.1–1998.12

	undiscounted				discounted			
	1978.1–1993.12		1994.1–1998.12		1978.1–1993.12		1994.1–1998.12	
	Estim	t-stat	Estim	t-stat	Estim	t-stat	Estim	t-stat
b_1	0.00	0.00	0.001	0.53	0.00	0.00	0.001	0.39
b_2	0.423	0.04	0.308	0.16	0.498	0.04	0.365	0.14
b_3	0.338	0.02	-0.200	-0.10	0.401	0.03	-0.266	-0.09
b_4	0.048	0.01	-0.318	-0.19	-0.062	-0.01	-0.548	-0.22
b_5	-0.042	-0.72	-0.203	-25.86	0.018	0.30	-0.061	-13.08
b_6	-0.025	-0.32	0.277	17.61	-0.086	-1.07	0.056	5.91

area that do not seem to be sustainable. Our tests imply there is a build-up of foreign assets that particularly occurred after the currency crisis 1992–1993.

In sum, we have shown, here, that sustainable debt in models with borrowing and lending may typically be state constrained. In order to control credit risk the lender needs to know the debt capacity of the borrower at each point in time. This knowledge seems to be necessary if one wants to move beyond an one period debt contract. We explore the problem of critical debt and creditworthiness by applying the Hamiltonian. Using those methods we analytically and numerically can demonstrate the region in which the borrower remains creditworthy. Imposing a ceiling on borrowing may lead to a loss of welfare if it is set to low. Moreover, in some instances it may be necessary for the borrower to first increase debt in order to decrease it. On the other hand, if the ceiling is set too high the non-explosiveness condition may not hold and creditworthiness may be lost.

By using this method we study the debt capacity of a borrower, the role of debt ceilings for lending and borrowing behavior.[48] The computation of these creditworthiness curves serves to determine sustainable debt for any initial capital stock k_0 and thus to control credit risk for any point in time. We note that there are, of course, numerous empirical approaches to control for credit risk by approximating sustainable debt by empirical indicators.[49] Our attempt was, however, to show how one can compute sustainable debt based on a dynamic economic model without having to refer to the numerous indicators for credit risk that rating companies use.

4.5 Conclusions

In this chapter we have undertaken some empirical tests on credit market and economic activity. After introducing some linear regression tests on bankruptcy risk and economic activity we have tested for nonlinear relationships in the financial-real interaction. Both types of tests have used US time series data. It seems to us that, in particular, nonlinear relationships are present in the short-run. These can be detected by looking at short time scales in the relationship between liquidity and output.

We then presented an intertemporal model with a credit market and applied it to an open economy problem where a country borrows from abroad. We estimate that model with time series data. We have managed to transform the dynamic model into an empirical model so that it can be taken to the data. Given the parameter estimates we can, for actual economies, compute the borrowing capacity and debt ceiling of actual countries that should hold for the long-run. This was undertaken for the core countries of the Euro-area. We have also shown that one can compute the sustainability of debt for actual economies by using time series methods. As it turns out the result for the Euro-area is that the Euro-area does not have liabilities but rather owns net assets vis-a-vis the rest of the world.[50]

Finally we note that our time series methods (Chap. 4.4.) to compute sustainable debt could be applied to any agent's debt. It could be a firm, a household, a government or country. An application of the above proposed time series methods to government debt is given in Greiner and Semmler (1999). Debt sustainability is an important issue in credit rating of private and sovereign debt and the above method can be applied to provide estimates of the long-run debt sustainability and credit risk.

---

[48] We also can show that multiple equilibria may arise if there are state dependent credit costs. The multiple equilibria may be important since there may be cut-off points which decide whether the economy moves to high or low level steady states.

[49] In a series of papers Milesi-Ferretti and Razin (1996, 1997, 1998) have addressed the empirical issue of how to obtain proxies for measuring sustainable debt.

[50] The implication of this computation is that the Euro as a currency should be rather stable in the long-run since currency runs should not be expected.

The Stock Market and Economic Activity

Chapter 5
Approaches to Stock Market
and Economic Activity

5.1 Introduction

The interaction of the stock market and economic activity has recently become an important topic in empirical finance as well as in macroeconomic research. The research has pursued two directions.

A large number of papers have studied the impact of the stock market on real activity. Here particular emphasis is given to the relationship of the volatility of the stock market and output. The research studies the impact of wealth, as evaluated on the stock market, on borrowing, lending and spending behavior of banks, firms and households. The argument may go like this. An increase in wealth through the appreciation of stocks increases spending directly since people feel wealthier. At the same time the appreciation of stocks increases the collateral for borrowing by firms and households. Credit may expand and thus spending is likely to increase. A depreciation of stocks lets spending decrease and devaluates the collateral and credit contractions followed by large output loss may occur. Thus, large stock price swings can easily be seen to impact economic activity. Often Tobin's Q is employed to study this impact of stock market appreciation or depreciation on firm investment. Of course, other financial variables such as interest rates, interest rate spreads, the term structure of the interest rates and credit constraints, as discussed in Chaps. 1–4 are also important for household and firm spending. Thus, beside the real variables, asset prices and financial variables are also important for economic activity and, moreover, have often been good predictors for turning points in economic activity and business cycles.[1]

On the other hand, another important line of research is to show how real activity affects asset prices and returns. Often, proxies for economic fundamentals are employed to show that fundamentals drive stock prices and returns. The two main important variables for stock prices are the expected cash flows (and dividend payments) of firms and discount rates. Both are supposed to determine asset prices in a fundamental way. Empirical researchers have used numerous macroeconomic variables as proxies for news on expected returns, future cash flows and discount rates.[2]

---

[1] For details of the role of financial variables as predictors for business cycles, see Friedman and Kuttner (1992), Stock and Watson (1989), Estrella and Hardouvilis (1991), Estrella and Mishkin (1997) and Plosser and Rouwenhorst (1994), Lettau and Ludvigson (2001 a,b, 2002).

[2] See Fama and French (1988), Fama and French (1989), Fama (1990).

In addition variables with leads and lags are studied for their impact on asset pricing and returns. In general, econometric literature has shown that good predictors of stock prices and returns have proved to be dividends, earnings and growth rate of real output[3] Moreover, financial variables such as interest rate spread and the term structure of interest rates have also been significant in predicting stock prices and stock returns (Fama (1990), Schwert (1990)). Other balance sheet variables, such as firms' leverage ratio, net worth and liquidity have also successfully been employed (Schwert 1990).

Presently discussed approaches in the empirical literature have primarily stressed either of the above mentioned two strands of research. Subsequently we will present some approaches, the relevant stylized facts for those approaches and some empirical results of the studies. Thereafter, we will present two models that deal with the interaction of macroeconomic factors and the stock market. We will also discuss some empirical results on such models as well.

5.2 The Intertemporal Approach

Currently, the best known approach is the market efficiency hypothesis. Theoretically it is based on the capital asset pricing model (CAPM) or consumption based capital asset pricing model (CCAPM). Details of these models will be presented in Chaps. 8–9. In terms of economic models researchers, nowadays, often employ a production based capital asset pricing model, a stochastic optimal growth model of RBC type, for studying the relationship between asset markets and real activity. Intertemporal decisions are at the heart of the RBC methodology and it is thus natural to study the asset market-output interaction in the context of such a model since it also includes production. Some advances have been made by using stochastic growth models to predict asset prices and returns. Here short summaries of stylized facts frequently cited in connection with this approach as well as a survey of empirical results, may suffice. Details are postponed to Chap. 10. The intertemporal equilibrium model is often measured against the stylized facts.

Recently it has become customary to contrast historical time series with a model's time series and to demonstrate to what extent the model's time series can match historical data. Models are required to match statistical regularities of actual time series in terms of the first and second moments and the cross correlation with output.

---

[3] See Fama and French (1988), Fama and French (1989), Fama (1990) and to some extent inflation rates, Schwert (1989).

[4] For the US real variables are measured in growth rates, 1970.1–1993.3. Data are taken from Canova and Nicola (1995). Asset market data represent real returns and are from Lettau, Gong and Semmler (2001) and represent 1947.1–1993.3. All data are of quarterly frequency. Asset market units are per cent per quarter. The T-bill rate is the 3 month T-bill rate. The Sharpe-ratio is the mean of equity divided by it's standard deviation. For Europe real variables are also measured in growth rates, 1970.1–1993.3. Data are taken from Eurostat (1997). Following Canova and Nicola (1995) for each of the variables a European variable is obtained by employing a weighted average of the respective variables for Germany, France, Italy and

Table 5.1. Stylized facts on real variables and asset markets: US and European data [4]

Variable	US		Europe	
	mean	std.dev.	mean	std.dev
GNP		0.97		0.65
Consumption		0.77		0.61
Investment		2.88		1.40
Employment		0.46		0.32
T-bill	0.18	0.86	0.43	0.89
Stock-return	2.17	7.53	1.81	7.37
Equity premium	1.99	7.42	1.38	7.04
Sharpe-ratio	0.27		0.19	

In the Table 5.1 we present summary statistics of time series for US and Europe on GNP, consumption, investment, employment, the treasury bill rate, equity return and the Sharpe-ratio. The latter measure of financial market performance has recently become a quite convenient measure to match theory and facts, since, as a measure of the risk-return trade-off, the Sharpe-ratio captures both excess returns and excess volatility.[5] Yet, we want to mention that the Sharpe-ratio might also be time varying. This will be discussed in Chaps. 9–10.

As shown in Table 5.1, the hierarchy of volatility measured by the standard deviation is common for US as well as European data. As shown, stock returns exhibit the strongest volatility. The second strongest volatility is exhibited by investment followed by consumption. Employment has the lowest volatility.

In addition, as can be seen for US as well as European data, the equity return carries an equity premium as compared to the risk free interest rate. This excess return was first stated by Mehra and Prescott (1985) as the equity premium puzzle. As can be observed the market return by far exceeds the return from the risk-free rate. As shown in a variety of recent papers,[6] the intertemporal models, in particular the RBC model insufficiently explains the equity premium and the excess volatility of equity return and thus the Sharpe-ratio. Standard RBC asset market models employ the Solow-residual as technology shocks – or impulse dynamics. For a given variance of the technology shock, standard utility functions and no adjustment costs, asset market facts are hard to match with the standard model. For details see Chap. 9.

---

the U.K, where GNP ratios are taken as the weight. This holds also for the 3 month T-bill rate. In the case of the U.K. the T-bill rate was obtained by averaging short term rates.

[5] See Lettau and Uhlig (1997 a,b) and Lettau, Gong and Semmler (2001) where the Sharpe-ratio is employed as a measure to match theory and facts in the financial market.

[6] See, for example, Rouwenhorst (1995), Danthin, Donaldson and Mehra (1992), Boldrin, Christiano and Fisher (1996, 2001), Lettau (1997), Lettau and Uhlig (1997) and Lettau, Gong and Semmler (2001).

In sum, for the actual time series compared, for example, with the standard RBC model, we observe a larger equity return and stronger volatility of equity prices in contrast to the risk-free rate. These two facts are measured by the Sharpe-ratio which cannot be matched by the standard RBC model.[7] Moreover, it is worth noting that in the stochastic growth model there is only a one-sided relationship. Real shocks affect stock prices and returns but shocks to asset prices – or overreaction of asset prices relative to changes in fundamentals – have no effects on real activity. The asset market is always cleared and there are no feedback mechanisms to propagate financial shocks to the real side.

The asset market implications of the above mentioned intertemporal models – and also the RBC model – are, for example, studied in Rouwenhorst (1995), Danthine, Donaldson and Mehra (1992), Lettau and Uhlig (1997 a,b), Lettau, Gong and Semmler (2001), Wöhrmann, Semmler and Lettau (2001) and Boldrin, Christiano and Fisher (2001). There, the baseline model with technology shocks as the driving force for macroeconomic fluctuations as well as some extensions of the base line model are employed to attempt to replicate the above summarized basic stylized facts of the stock market such as the excess volatility of asset prices and returns, the excess return,[8] the spread between asset returns the risk-free rate, and the Sharpe-ratio. The general result is that the baseline model has failed to replicate the above stylized facts. Details for both consumption as well as production based asset pricing models are evaluated in chs.9-10. As mentioned above, there are numerous extensions that have been developed to overcome some of the deficiencies of the representative agent model to asset pricing. Some success can be found in a recent attempt by Boldrin, Christiano and Fisher (2001).

5.3 The Excess Volatility Theory

Other theories and macro econometric studies depart from the market efficiency hypothesis and pursue the overreaction hypothesis when employing macro variables as predictors for stock prices and stock returns (Shiller 1991, Summers 1986, Poterba and Summers 1988). Moreover, in this tradition the role of monetary, fiscal and external shocks are seen to be relevant. Although in the long run stock prices may revert to their mean as determined by macroeconomic proxies of fundamentals in the short-run, speculative forces and the interaction of trading strategies of heterogenous agents may be more relevant than fundamentals. The latter view has been, with some success, tested in the mean reversion hypothesis of Poterba and Summers (1988).[9]

---

[7]Danthine et al. who study the equity return also state:"To the equity premium and risk free rate puzzles, we add an excess volatility puzzle: the essential inability of the RBC model to replicate the observation that the market rate of return is fundamentally more volatile than the national product"(Danthine et.al. 1992: 531).

[8]See Mehra and Prescott (1985).

[9]The overreaction of equity prices in relation to news on fundamentals originates, in this view, in positive feedback mechanisms operating in financial markets. Details are discussed in Chap. 5.4.

Let us use the following notations: p, the real S&P composite stock price index, and p^* the ex post rational expectations price (detrended by a exponential growth factor).[10]

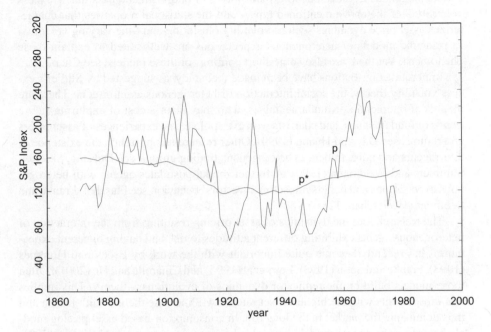

Fig. 5.1. Excess volatility

Shiller (1991) has devised an empirical test of the "present value model" with "constant discount rate". There he defines "excess volatility". He uses a variance bound test such as

$$\sigma(D) \geq \sqrt{2r}\sigma(\Delta p).$$

This variance bound test means that the standard deviation must be at least $\sigma(D)$ to justify the volatility of stock prices. Take, for example, $r = 0.07$; $\sigma(\Delta p) = 8.2$; $\sigma(D)$ must be 3.07; but $\sigma(D)$ is only 0.76 for the data Shiller employs.

Recently, because of some criticism of using a constant discount rate, the excess volatility theory has been extended and researchers have used stochastic discount factors, see Shiller (1991). For details of this criticism and discussions on time varying discount rates, see Cochrane (2001, Chap. 21). Still the basic puzzle, namely the excess volatility remains. A study of excess volatility of the stock price for an industry is undertaken in Mazzucato and Semmler (1999).

---

[10]For the methodology of how to compute the ex post rational expectation price, see Shiller (1991). The data are from http://www.econ.yale.edu/~shiller/data.htm

5.4 Heterogenous Agents Models

In recent times numerous researchers have developed models of heterogenous agents and heterogenous expectations to explain waves of optimism and pessimism, excess volatility – of the above mentioned type – and the statistical properties that characterizes asset price dynamics such as volatility clustering and time varying volatility. In principle models of heterogenous expectations are well suited to explain those phenomena. Yet there are also some short comings of those models, see Chap. 7.

Important contributions have been made that study, as suggested by Shiller's excess volatility theory, the social interaction of heterogenous asset traders. There are models of interaction of fundamentalists, who may incur a cost of exploring future trends of fundamentals, and chartists who extrapolate past experiences of asset prices and returns, see Day and Huang (1990). Other researchers postulate the existence of arbitrageurs and noise traders as heterogenous trading groups, see DeLong, Shleifer, Summers and Waldmann (1990). A further model postulates agents with heterogenous expectations and beliefs impacting investors' behavior, see Flaschel, Franke and Semmler (1997, Chap. 12).

The research into the dynamics of asset pricing resulting from the interaction of heterogenous agents exhibiting different attitudes to risk and having different expectations has recently become quite important with the work by Brock and Hommes (1998), Franke and Sethi (1998), Levy et al (1995) and Chiarella and He (2001). Often those models build on the replicator dynamics of evolutionary theory. This implies that those agents with the highest asset returns will increase there wealth fastest and thus dominante the market in the long run. In consumption-based asset pricing models heterogenous agents models have also become important, see Cochrane (2001, Chap. 21).

Such models are elegantly summarized in a recent work by Chiarella and He (2001). A stylized model of this type may read as follows. The expected return is defined as

$$E_t(\rho_{t+1}) = r + \delta + d\bar{\rho}_t$$

with $E_t(\rho_{t+1})$ the expected return on an asset, δ the equity premium, here taken as a constant, and, d the weight of the chartists, who may be trend followers $(d > 0)$ or contrarians $(d < 0)$ and

$$\bar{\rho}_t = \frac{1}{L} \sum_{k=1}^{L} \rho_{t-k},$$

the expected trend formulated by the chartists and contrarians. The variance of the return, $V(\rho_{t+1})$, may be time varying. The expected return by the fundamentalist investors $r + \delta$, is assumed to be constant, with r the risk-free interest rate and δ the equity premium and thus for the fundamentalists holds $d = 0$. Chiarella and He (2001) extend the model by allowing each group of agents to perceive specific equity primia such that one can have different δ_i for each group of agents.

The wealth proportions of the different types of investors evolve over time, depending on their relative success in predicting the return. The model can replicate, depending on the parameters chosen, the above mentioned statistical properties of actual asset markets such as volatility clustering and thus time varying variance, but since the equity premium is given exogenously the model does not attempt to replicate the equity premium or the Sharpe-ratio which empirically also appears to be time varying. An attempt to study the forces determining the (constant) equity premium and Sharpe-ratio is made in Chap. 6 and by the approaches studied in Chaps. 9–10.

Moreover, although the heterogenous trading strategies of the different groups of investors may generate overshooting and quite complex asset price dynamics, we want to point out that it is presumably the interaction of the trading strategies and the varying perception of what the fundamentals are – and what their trend is – which explains the actual asset price dynamics. A model of this type is discussed in Chap. 7.

5.5 The VAR Methodology

In general it is well recognized that the studies of the interaction of financial and real variables have difficulties in fully capturing the lead and lag patterns in financial and real variables when tested econometrically. To overcome this deficiency, the use of the VAR framework to test for lead and lag patterns has been appealing. A first application of a VAR methodology to European data sets can be found in Canova and Nichola (1995).

Employing a VAR on stock price, interest rate and output (using a linear structure of the model for US time series data 1960.1–1993.10), Chiarella, Semmler and Mittnik (2002) obtain results as depicted in the following figure. Figure 5.2 shows the cumulative impulse-responses for US time series data 1960.01–1993.10 with the three variables: output (growth rates of the monthly production index, Prod), real T-bill (monthly T-bill, TB) and monthly real stock price (nominal stock price deflated by the consumer price index, ST). The solid lines are the impulse responses and the broken lines the error bands.

Overall, we can summarize the following results: A one standard deviation shock to output has a positive effect in the next periods and keeps output persistently up. The T-bill rises and the stock prices falls. This is the direction of change in real and financial variables that one would expect. On the other hand a shock to the T-bill keeps the T-bill up and there is, as one also would expect, a fall in the stock price. Yet, the output is only insignificantly affected (and also has the wrong sign). If there is a shock to the stock price, the stock price is persistently higher, yet the T-bill and output are only insignificantly affected.

Overall, a shock to output is affecting output and may impact the interest rate and stock price with a delay. Concerning the interest rate, the T-Bill, one usually expects an immediate impact effect on the stock prices and on output with a delay. We see in the above study a very small effect (yet of incorrect sign) but this may come from the fact that output, as discussed in Chap. 2, will most likely respond to long-term interest

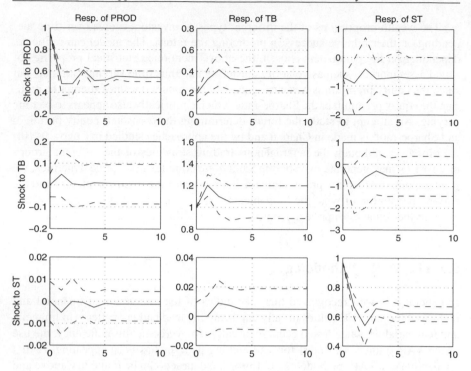

Fig. 5.2. Cumulative impulse-responses

rates and less to short-term interest rates. On the other hand, we correctly see what one would expect that a shock to the stock price affects the stock price, but output and interest rates are only marginally or not affected. This appears to hold at least in linear VAR studies. Yet one might want to predict that if there is a large shock to stock prices, as, for example, the shock of October 1987 in the US and the stock market shock 1997–98 in Asian countries, the effects on output may be larger. In linear VAR studies the response is always proportional to shocks and the effects of large shocks – shocks beyond a certain threshold initiating credit contractions and bank failures – cannot be captured. This can be studied in threshold models and models that also take into account other financial markets. A study of this type is pursued in Chap. 12. Moreover, a more complete VAR study of the stock market and its interaction with other variables may also take into account inflation rates and exchange rates.

Overall, one might argue that the VAR methodology is strong in capturing lead and lag patterns in the interaction of the variables but it does not reveal important structural relations, in particular if nonlinearities prevail in the interaction of the variables. Moreover, dynamic macro models may be needed to provide some rationale for the use of structural relationships and to highlight relevant restrictions on empirical tests. This is undertaken in Chap. 6.

5.6 Regime Change Models

There is some econometric work on the nonlinear interaction of stock market and output. The major type of models are built on Hamilton's regime change models. The Hamilton idea (Hamilton, 1989) that output follows two different autoregressive processes depending on whether the economy is in an expanding or contracting regime, is extended to a study of the stock market in Hamilton and Lin (1996).[11] Connecting to the above work by Schwert it is presumed that periods of high volatility may interchange with periods of low volatility of stock returns depending on whether the economy is in a recession or expansion. On the other hand, an important factor for the output at business cycle frequency appears to be the state of the stock market. In their version Hamilton and Lin (1996) show some predictive power embedded in the stock market for output and conversely, using a regime change model, the state of the economy as predictor for the volatility of stock returns.

The fact that the volatility is following two different regimes – recessions and expansions– is documented in the following figure where the space between the broken and dotted lines indicates recessions.

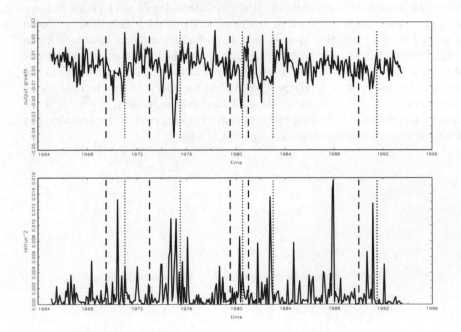

Fig. 5.3. Volatility regimes

In the lower part of the figure, where the squared returns are shown, we can nicely observe that volatility of stock returns follows two different regimes.

---

[11]For further regime change models, see Rothman (1999).

Another nonlinear test for stock prices and output can be undertaken by using the STR methodology as introduced in Chap. 4.3 for liquidity and output. One can obtain interesting results using a bivariate STR estimate, for details, see Chiarella, Semmler and Koçkesen (1998). There, a delayed stock price acts as threshold for the output variable and a delayed output variable acts as threshold for the stock price.

The above mentioned studies of threshold (or business cycle) dependent volatility points to the possibility that returns and volatility may not be constant but time varying, i.e. vary with the business cycle. This gives rise to the conjecture that the above stated assumption in Chap. 5.2 of a constant risk-free rate, equity premium and Sharpe-ratio – often referred to in RBC models – might not be quite correct. One should rather attempt to match models with time varying financial characteristics such as the risk-free rate, equity premium and Sharpe-ratio. This is, with some success, undertaken in Wöhrmann and Semmler and Lettau (2001).

5.7 Conclusions

Our review of empirical approaches to study the interaction of stock prices and output – or in some cases stock prices, other financial variables and output – should be viewed as an introduction to modelling asset markets and economic activity. In Chap. 6 macro factors impacting stock prices are studied and a macro model that takes account of the interaction of macro variables and asset prices is introduced and empirical results reported. In Chap. 7 we explore the effects of new technology on asset prices and returns. Thereafter standard asset pricing models, in particular the capital asset pricing and intertemporal capital asset pricing models, are considered in detail and some estimation results are reported as well.

Chapter 6
Macro Factors and the Stock Market

6.1 Introduction

Dynamic macro models of Keynesian type can be used to explain the interaction of stock prices, interest rates and output. Such an approach has been introduced by Blanchard (1981) where he studies the interaction of stock price, interest rate and aggregate activity. In the Blanchard (1981) model, unlike in the RBC model, there are in principle, cross effects between asset prices and real activity. Along the line of Tobin (1969, 1980) it is presumed that output, through consumption and investment functions, is driven by real activity as well as stock prices. Output demand is determined by consumption and investment behaviors. As empirical studies have shown a contemporaneous relation of investment and the stock price may be weak. Yet, when lags are introduced and Tobin's Q is measured as marginal Q, as some studies do (Abel and Blanchard 1984), or the discount factor is approximated by a time varying risk premium (Lettau and Ludvigson, 2001), the relationship appears to improve.

On the other hand, since the Blanchard macro model is in a sense, a rational expectations model, shocks to macroeconomic variables cause stock prices to jump whilst keeping the output fixed (rather than allowing it to adjust gradually). Thus because stock prices jump there is still no feedback effect on output. Once the stock price is on the stable branch output also gradually adjusts.[1] The stock price overshoots its steady state value during its jump and then decreases thereafter. Blanchard's macro model thus predicts that unless unanticipated shocks occur, the stock price moves monotonically toward a point of rest or if it is there it will stay there. In fact, only exogenous shocks will move stock prices. This line of research has been, as above mentioned, econometrically pursued in papers by Summers (1986), Cutler, Poterba and Summers (1989) and McMillin and Laumas (1988). As in other rational expectations models, in its basic version, feedback mechanisms still do not exist that can lead to an endogenous propagation of shocks and fluctuations.

Below the Blanchard model will appropriately be modified to allow for such feedback effects. We modify and extend the Blanchard model and econometrically

---

[1] Blanchard states: "Following a standard if not entirely convincing practice, I shall assume that q always adjusts so as to leave the economy on the stable path to the equilibrium" (Blanchard 1981:135); see also p. 136 where Blanchard discusses the response of the stock price to shocks, for example, unanticipated monetary and fiscal shocks. For a detailed discussion on policy shocks in the context of the Blanchard model, see McMillin and Laumas (1988).

study the interaction of stock price, interest rate and output. The Blanchard variant is as mentioned, a perfect foresight model which exhibits saddle path stability. In Chiarella, Semmler, Mittnik and Zhu (2002) the perfect foresight jump variable technique is replaced by gradual adjustments, in particular gradual expectations adjustments based on adaptive expectations. The limiting behavior of such a model which admits, among others, cyclical paths generates the Blanchard model when expectations adjust infinitely fast to yield perfect foresight as a limiting case.[2] The model is solved through discrete time approximation and empirically estimated for time series data.

Based on the Blanchard variant[3] in this chapter a modelling strategy is pursued for the relationship of stock market, interest rate and real activity that overcomes weaknesses of both the RBC model and the rational expectations version of a macro model. In our model, unlike in the RBC type stochastic growth model, the stock price will impact the real activity, and different from the Blanchard model, stock price jumps to their stable paths are avoided by positing gradual adjustments of stock prices, interest rates and output. This, in turn, may better explain the endogenous propagation mechanism and fluctuations of both stock prices and output.

6.2 A Dynamic Macro Model

In our notations, we follow Blanchard (1981). Output prices are fixed. q is an index of the stock price, y is output, g the index of fiscal expenditure, d is aggregate expenditure

$$d = aq + \beta y + g \quad (a > 0, \quad 0 \leq \beta < 1). \tag{6.1}$$

Output adjusts to changes in aggregate expenditure with a delay according to

$$\dot{y} = \kappa_y(d - y)$$
$$= \kappa_y(aq - by + g), \tag{6.2}$$

where $b \equiv 1 - \beta$ so that $0 < b < 1$ and the speed of output adjustment $\kappa_y > 0$.

From the standard assumption of an LM-equilibrium in the asset market we can write

$$i = cy - h(m - p) \quad (c > 0, h > 0), \tag{6.3}$$

where i denotes the short term rate of interest, m and p the logarithms of nominal money and prices respectively.

Real profit is given by

$$\pi = \alpha_0 + \alpha_1 y, \tag{6.4}$$

---

[2]Further models of this macroeconomic modelling tradition that include the financial market can be found in Flaschel, Franke and Semmler (1997).

[3]The subsequent section is based on Chiarella, Semmler, Mittnik and Zhu, (2002).

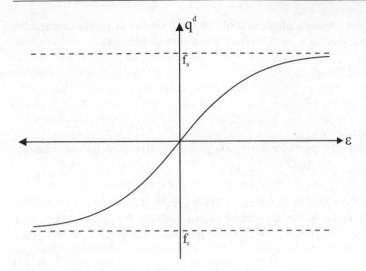

Fig. 6.1. Excess demand for stock

so that $(x + \alpha_0 + \alpha_1 y)/q$ is the instantaneous expected real rate of return from holding shares, x denotes the expected change in the value of the stock market. Hence the excess return is (which may allow for a constant risk premium on equity, see below)

$$\epsilon = \frac{x + \alpha_0 + \alpha_1 y}{q} - i. \tag{6.5}$$

In Blanchard ϵ is always zero. This assumes perfect substitutes and no arbitrage is possible. With imperfect substitutability between the two assets, the excess demand for stocks (q^d) is a positive but bounded function

$$q^d = f(\epsilon) \quad (f(0) = 0), \tag{6.6}$$

with f as in the following figure.

If we allow for an equity premium, as discussed in Chap. 5, $\bar{\epsilon}$, with the equity premium a constant this would give rise to

$$q^d = f(\epsilon - \bar{\epsilon}) \quad (f(0) = -\bar{\epsilon}),$$

instead of (6.6) and the function, as depicted in the above figure, would shift to the left.

We further assume that the stock market adjusts to the excess demand according to

$$\dot{q} = \kappa_q f(\epsilon) \text{ or} \tag{6.7}$$

$$\dot{q} = \kappa_q f(\epsilon - \bar{\epsilon}) \tag{6.8}$$

where $\kappa_q (> 0)$ is the speed of adjustment of the stock market to excess demand for stocks. If we assume that $\kappa_q = \infty$ then from the above we recover

$$\frac{x + \alpha_0 + \alpha_1 y}{q} = i, \text{ or} \tag{6.9}$$

$$\frac{x + \alpha_0 + \alpha_1 y}{q} = i + \bar{\epsilon} \tag{6.10}$$

the Blanchard model.

For the formation of expectations we assume the adaptive expectations scheme.

$$\dot{x} = \kappa_x (\dot{q} - x), \tag{6.11}$$

where $\kappa_x (> 0)$ is the speed of revisions to expectations. The inverse κ_x^{-1} may be interpreted as the time lag in the adjustment of expectations. By assuming this time lag to be zero (i.e. $\kappa_x = \infty$) the above equation reduces to the perfect foresight case

$$x = \dot{q}, \tag{6.12}$$

which is also a key assumption in Blanchard's model.

The generalized Blanchard model as worked out in Chiarella, Semmler, Mittnik and Zhu (2002) consists of

$$\dot{y} = \kappa_y (aq - by + g), \tag{6.13}$$

$$\dot{q} = \kappa_q \left(\frac{x + \alpha_0 + \alpha_1 y}{q} - cy + h(m - p) \right), \tag{6.14}$$

$$\dot{x} = \kappa_x \kappa_q f \left(\frac{x + \alpha_0 + \alpha_1 y}{q} - cy + h(m - p) \right) - x \right) \tag{6.15}$$

or with the equity premium $\bar{\epsilon}$

$$\dot{y} = \kappa_y (aq - by + g), \tag{6.16}$$

$$\dot{q} = \kappa_q f \left(\frac{x + \alpha_0 + \alpha_1 y}{q} - cy + h(m - p) - \bar{\epsilon} \right), \tag{6.17}$$

$$\dot{x} = \kappa_x \left(\kappa_q f \left(\frac{x + \alpha_0 + \alpha_1 y}{q} - cy + h(m - p) - \bar{\epsilon} \right) - x \right). \tag{6.18}$$

The equilibrium of the system is given by

$$\dot{y} = 0, \dot{q} = 0, \dot{x} = 0 \tag{6.19}$$

and the values $(\bar{y}, \bar{q})$ that solve

$$aq - by + g = 0,$$
$$\frac{\alpha_0 + \alpha_1 y}{q} = cy - h(m - p) \qquad \text{or}$$
$$aq - by + g = 0,$$
$$\frac{\alpha_0 + \alpha_1 y}{q} = cy - h(m - p) + \bar{\epsilon}.$$

Without the equity premium we will write $\delta \equiv h(m - p)$. For time varying real balances we denote $\delta_t = h(m_t - p_t)$ and with equity premium we may redefine $\delta_t = h(m_t - p_t) - \bar{\epsilon}$.

For the above system we first show how the original Blanchard model can be recovered from it. First we assume perfect foresight by letting $\kappa_x \to \infty$ which by the above yields

$$\dot{q} = x. \tag{6.20}$$

Then we assume instantaneous adjustment to excess demand in the stock market by letting $\kappa_q \to \infty$ in the above. Hence with no equity premium we obtain

$$\frac{x + \alpha_0 + \alpha_1 y}{q} = cy - h(m - p). \tag{6.21}$$

Combining the last two equations yields the differential equation for q

$$\dot{q} = q[cy - h(m - p)] - \alpha_0 - \alpha_1 y. \tag{6.22}$$

The differential equations for y and q constitute the dynamical system studied by Blanchard. The equilibria from the above system are saddle points in this perfect foresight case. If the jump-variable procedure which is used by Blanchard is not adopted then the global dynamics need to be considered. This means that we have to study the above three dimensional system, see Chiarella, Semmler, Mittnik and Zhu (2002). This system can be transformed into an estimable two dimensional system. It is then estimated in Chiarella, Semmler, Mittnik and Zhu (2002).

6.3 Empirical Results

When the system with three variables is transformed into a system with two variables we can directly estimate the nonlinear bivariate system by NLLS estimation using the Euler approximation method. We undertake this for US data 1960.01–1993.10.[4] In Chiarella, Semmler, Mittnik and Zhu (2002) we also present estimations for European Data (1974:02–1993.06).

We directly estimate the parameters of a discrete time nonlinear bivariate system with a constrained number of lags by using the Euler scheme. The estimated parameters, obtained from the BP- filtered data, are reported in Table 6.1. Direct estimation, using the Euler scheme for the transformed system (6.13)–(6.15) in bivariate form, are as follows:

---

[4]Results of a regime change model of STR type with an unconstrained lag structure are undertaken in Chiarella, Semmler and Koçkesen (1998) and compared to the direct estimation below.

Table 6.1. Parameter estimates, US: 1960.01–1993.10, detrended data [5]

Economic Structure	Speeds of Adjustment	Government Policy
$a = 0.122$	$\kappa_y = 0.185$	$g = 0.000$
$b = 0.370$	$\kappa_q = 0.240$	$\delta = -6.670$
$\alpha_0 = 0.065$	$\kappa_x = 1.120$	
$\alpha_1 = 6.620$		
$c = 1.568$		
$\lambda = 0.036$		
$\bar{f} = 0.205$		

Table 6.2. Parameter estimates, US: 1960.01–1993.10, detrended data [6]

Economic Structure	Speeds of Adjustment	Government Policy
$a = 0.122$	$\kappa_y = 0.285$	$g = 0.000$
$b = 0.370$	$\kappa_q = 1.998$	
$\alpha_0 = 0.397$	$\kappa_x = 1.798$	
$\alpha_1 = 0.05$		
$c = 0.400$		
$h = 0.100$		
$\bar{f} = 0.025$		
$\bar{\epsilon} = 0.035$		

It is noticeable from Table 6.1 that all parameters have the predicted sign, except δ which is estimated without the equity premium. Note also that δ is taken as a constant. One can observe the hierarchy in the speed of adjustments that also other studies would suggest. Since here the term $\delta = h(m - p)$ is fixed. We next take the time series of real balances $\delta_t = h(m_t - p_t)$ as exogenous sequence.[7] This assumes that the history of monetary policy is important, in that it affects m_t, for the path of interest rates. In addition, we account for a term that indicates an equity premium. We here posit that the equity premium is a constant showing up as a parameter in the model. The results with real balances and an equity premium are presented in Table 6.2. For this purpose the system (6.16)–(6.18) has also been transformed into an estimable bivariate system.[8]

---

[5] We employ monthly data on stock price and an index of industrial production which are taken from the Hamilton and Lin (1996) data set.
[6] In the estimations above we have prefixed c and h.
[7] The data for money M and price level P are obtained from Citibase (1998).
[8] For details see Chiarella, Semmler, Mittnik and Zhu (2002).

Here, too, all parameters are reasonable and the hierarchy of adjustment speeds is reasonable as well. There is now an equity premium, $\bar{\epsilon}$, which has the expected sign, although, since we have used detrended data, the size of it is hard to interpret.

Overall the direct estimation of the model performs reasonably well. Moreover, in Chiarella, Semmler, Mittnik and Zhu (2002) stochastic simulations with the estimated parameters of Table 6.2 are reported that show that this type of dynamic macro model can explain reasonably well the excess volatility of the stock price, the equity premium and the Sharpe-ratio.

6.4 Conclusions

The above suggested model that links the stock market, interest rates and output can be seen as a prototype model to understand the interaction of asset prices and real activity in modern economies. The model is still rudimentary in the sense that it lacks price dynamics, the term structure of interest rates, the effects of monetary monetary and fiscal policies and the impact of exchange rate fluctuations on both stock prices and output (see Chap. 12). Yet, such a type of model can be considered as a working model for numerous extensions. For further variants of this type of model, see Chiarella, Flaschel and Semmler (2001). However, in the above model there is still no evolution of new technology that may impact both asset prices as well as output. A model of the stock market including the latter is presented next.

Chapter 7
New Technology and the Stock Market

7.1 Introduction

In the previous model there was no evolution of new technologies that could impact productivity, output and asset prices. Recent models explicitly consider the relationship between new technology and stock prices, see (Greenwood and Jovanovic (1999), Hobijn and Jovanovic (1999) and Mazzucato and Semmler (1999, 2002)). This type of work studies the effect of the evolution of new technologies on stock prices. The main hypothesis here is that the perceived emergence of new technology makes the asset price of existing technology, operated by incumbents, fall and the asset price of the innovators, the newcomers, rise.

7.2 Some Facts

The fall of the aggregate stock price in the 1980s and then the rapid rise of the stock price in the 1990s in the US has often been used as an historical example to exemplify those two opposing effects of new technology on stock prices. Greenwood and Jovanovic (1999) show that the stock price of the incumbents first fell in the 1970s and then remained flat in the 1980s and 1990s whereas the stock price of all firms, driven by the innovators, has been rising since the end of the 1980s.

Next we may look at the investment into new technology and stock prices. Figure 7.1 shows the share of information technology investment of total investment in equipment and the rise of the Nasdaq in the 1990s. As Greenwood and Jovanovic (1999) show the Nasdaq was mainly driven by new IT start up firms. As Fig. 7.1, which is based on the data by Hobijn and Jovanovic (1999), demonstrates there is a strong comovement of the Nasdaq and investment new technology.

Greenwood and Jovanovic (1999) and Hobijn and Jovanovic (1999) use the Lucas (1978) consumption-based asset price model in order to explain the phenomena depicted in Fig. 7.1. In their model, however, there are no firms, and the dividend payments are exogenously given as in the Lucas (1978) model.

The following model, developed by Semmler and Greiner (1996), starts with firms and earnings of firms and may be more suitable for understanding such periods of major technological change and the associated stock price movements. At the center of this model are two types of firms, incumbent firms and innovators. Whereas the

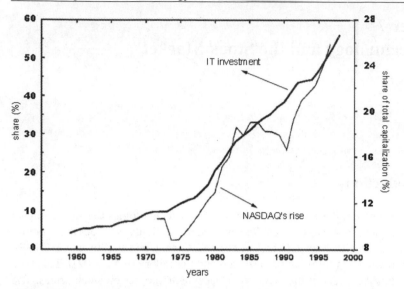

Fig. 7.1. Nasdaq stock price and investment in computer equipment

incumbent firms cling to old technologies, at least for a while, it takes time until the innovators add value to the stock market.

In the model one group of firms is presumed to actively innovate and the other group, the incumbents who operate existing technology, passively respond to changes in the technological environment. Innovating firms usually expect a return from committing resources and undertaking inventive investment. They may compute the net present value of their revenue from the innovation. While the innovators aim at capturing excess profit when the technology is implemented, the second group, the incumbents, may, under competitive pressure, learn to improve their efficiency and profit by being second movers. We posit that the new technology will be created at a certain cost, an innovation cost. The total cost for operating the new technology is assumed to be dependent on the effort spent to obtain the new technology (independent of the number of firms) and a cost proportional to the number of firms operating it.

We do not, however, presume that perfectly competitive conditions hold so that the profit for the innovators is instantly dissipating. It is reasonable to presume that the new technology is employed monopolistically. When the innovators expect gains from innovations – which can be expressed as the present value of future profit flows – the innovating firms will expand. While anticipation of the innovators earnings make stock prices rise the perceived out-dated vintages of capital goods of the incumbents make their stock prices fall. Although, there might be entry into the group of innovating firms, encouraged by excess profits, there may also be occuring exits due to negative profits, see Hobijn and Jovanovic (1999). We might assume that the process of compressing the profit is slow.

By borrowing from evolutionary theory we may assume different types of interaction effects between the firms: a *predator-prey* relation between the innovators and incumbents, a *cooperative effect*; and a *competition (or crowding) effect*. The predator-prey relation occurs when innovators grow at the expense of the incumbents. The competitive effect results when the new technology dissipates. The excess profit falls because of reduced prices and compressed mark-ups. We may use an inverse demand function to specify this effect. A cooperative effect (spillover or learning effect) bounds the number of incumbents away from zero, so that, although firms exit, complete extinction of incumbents does not occur. With a costly new technology, the innovators most likely will have an unprofitable period when the new technology is introduced and thus the stock price will not rise yet. On the other hand, the forward looking stock market may anticipate net income gains and stock prices may rise. Innovative firms face a period when they can enjoy technological rent and rising stock prices. Later, firms may lose their profit due to the subsequent competitive effect as a result of an increase in the capacity to produce and the incumbents capability to adopt the new technology.

7.3 The Model

A small scale model of two types of firms modelling the behavior of the innovators and the incumbents is posited

$$V_{\max} = \int_0^\infty e^{-rt} g(x_2, u) dt; u \in \Omega_+$$

s.t.

$$\dot{x}_1 = k - ax_1 x_2^2 + bx_2 - x_1 e/\mu \tag{7.1}$$

$$\dot{x}_2 = x_2(ax_1 x_2 + vg(x_2, u) - \beta) \tag{7.2}$$

with $g(x_2, u) = \mu(x_2, u)x_2 u - cu - c_0 x_2$, $\mu = \alpha/(\Phi + x_2 u)$, where $k, \alpha, \beta, e, c, \Phi$ and $v > 0$ are constants, x_1 is the number of incumbents, x_2 the number of innovators and u a decision variable related to the introduction of new technology. The decision variable u indicates the level of effort spent to create the new technology. This can mean the hiring of engineers, running research laboratories or purchasing information on new technologies. This investment is usually risky since there is considerable uncertainty and risk involved. We limit our model to a deterministic version.[1]

The cost per unit of effort is denoted by c. The cost cu is independent of the number of firms and there is a cost proportional to the number of firms, $c_0 x_2$. Thus, $cu + c_0 x_2$ is the amount of resources that innovators have to devote to the innovation. The term $\mu(\cdot)$ is the (net) price, or markup, received for the product produced by the new technology, where $\mu(\cdot)x_2 u$ is the net revenue. When the innovators attempt to

---

[1]For a stochastic version, see Semmler (1994).

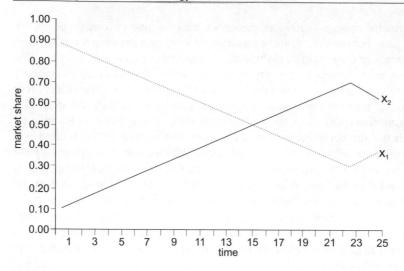

Fig. 7.2. Market share dynamics of innovators and incumbents

maximize the earnings arising from new technology $g(\cdot)$, facing a revenue $\mu(\cdot)x_2u$ and the cost $cu + c_0x_2$ excess profit will increase their number. In Eq. (7.2) the term $vg(\cdot)$ with v a constant, means that there is an increase in the number of innovators which is proportional to their excess profit.

The term $ax_1x_2^2$ represents the predator-prey interaction where the adoption of the new technology is supposed to take place proportionally to the product of x_1 and x_2x_2 (a common assumption for the spread of information in sales-advertising models). This implies that as the number of firms applying the new technology grows, so does the accessibility to that technology for the incumbents as well. This way the rate of decrease of the incumbents in (7.1) may be translated into an increase of the innovators in Eq. (7.2).

It is reasonable to posit that information about the new technology leaks out faster the larger the number of firms that apply the new technology. Our assumption means that the diffusion speed accelerates by x_2. The term bx_2 in Eq. (7.1) reflects the cooperative effect of x_2 on x_1. This represents learning by the incumbents to improve their performance when information about the new technology spreads and the competitive pressure from the new technology on the incumbents increases. The last term x_1e/μ in (7.1) is the crowding effect for x_1, with μ the mark-up from an inverse demand function which also appears in Eq. (7.2). [2]

Figure 7.2 depicts the relative market shares of the incumbents, x_1 and the innovators x_2, for certain initial conditions. It shows that innovating firms that undertake

---

[2]Semmler and Greiner (1996) show that there might be multiple equilibria of the model depending on parameters.

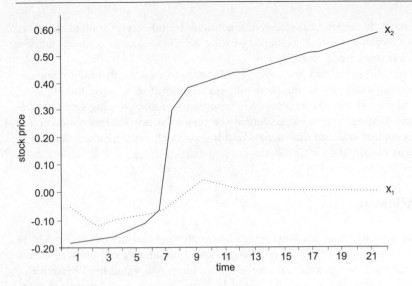

Fig. 7.3. Stock price dynamics of innovators and incumbents

an optimal inventive investment may succeed and increase their market share, but the incumbents still coexist side by side with the innovators operating the new technology. They may even gain back some market share at a later period.

In Fig. 7.3 the present value of the incumbents (dashed line) and the innovators (solid line) are depicted. The stock price of the incumbents is obtained by discounting their current profit flows and the innovators' stock price is obtained solving the model of equs. (7.1)–(7.2).[3]

Figures 7.2 and 7.3 replicate the aforementioned stylized facts on the innovators' expansion of the market share, the rise of its stock price, the long-run upswing of the innovators' stock price and the decline and low level of the incumbents' stock price due to the fact that they are technologically lagging. They also may cease to be valued by the financial market. This is what seems to have happened in the US in the 1980s and 1990s.

An analysis similar to ours on innovative effort, market share and stock price dynamics for the US can be found in Greenwood and Jovanovic (1999) and Hobijn and Jovanovic (1999). Yet, as aforementioned they are using a consumption-based asset pricing model, the Lucas (1978) asset price model. An asset price model of the above type that includes production is employed in Mazzucato and Semmler (2002) where

---

[3] Value function iteration using dynamic programming is employed to solve the above model, see Semmler and Greiner (1996). There it is also shown that, if the start-up cost for the innovator is too high compared to the expected returns, the innovator may end up with a negative present value and thus may go bankrupt.

the stock price dynamics of the early US automobile industry is studied. In either case such a dynamic view of technology evolution allows one to connect industry dynamics and stock price volatility.

In general, as Hobijn and Jovanovic (1999) have shown firms that fail to innovate successfully may fall prey to the more successful innovators – being the object of mergers and acquisitions -or are forced to exit, possibly leading to a large exit (shake-out) of firms. While stock prices may already be very volatile in the innovation period where it is unclear who are the winners and losers, stock price of firms that fail to innovate may rapidly drop after a shake-out and exits of firms.

7.4 Conclusions

Overall, we want to stress that long swings and short run volatility of stock prices in an economy with rapid technological change cannot be interpreted solely as excess volatility resulting, for example, from the mood, the strategy and herd behavior of stock market traders, as we have discussed in Chap. 5.3, but real determinants are important as well when a new technology arises. It is the turnover of the leading firms, the uncertain prospects of firms, their innovative potentials, the fluctuations in real earnings and dividends and the market share instability that are also strongly driving stock market volatility. Given those uncertainties about the real winners and losers there is excess volatility and occasional under- and over-valuation of the firm's, the industry's and economy's aggregate stock price.[4] Yet, as shown in Chap. 5.3, waves of optimism or pessimism are important in this context as well. In the interaction of heterogenous traders' social psychology becomes important when the fundamentals are uncertain in the presence of rapid technological change. Those waves of optimism or pessimism are neglected in some recent studies that propose that stock prices are driven solely by fundamentals (see Hobijn and Jovanovic, 1999).

---

[4]For a reasonable method to separate the volatility component that is driven by "fundamentals" and the excess volatility resulting, for example, from overoptimism or pessimism or from the psychology and social interaction of traders in a very uncertain environment, see Mazzucato and Semmler (1999).

Part IV

Asset Pricing and Economic Activity

Chapter 8
Portfolio Theory: CAPM and Extensions

8.1 Introduction

This chapter discusses theoretical foundations and empirical evidence for the most prominent asset pricing theory: the Capital Asset Pricing Model (CAPM). It represents a pricing model for risky assets. The CAPM has been extended to the multi-factor model (MFM) and arbitrage pricing theory (APT). The motivation of the latter has been to overcome the problems associated with the market portfolio in the CAPM by introducing a multi-factor approach. The subsequent chapter is kept simple and refers to the CAPM only. In some additional remarks crucial assumptions regarding investors' preferences and stock return distributions are relaxed. Currently the debate whether exact pricing restrictions in the MFM and APT imply the return to the "good old CAPM" is still going on. By introducing state dependent relationships as well as general nonlinearities in a CAPM model one can try to unify the different views but we will not elaborate on such extensions.

8.2 Portfolio Theory and CAPM: Simple Form

First we want to give some definitions. We denote by V_1 the portfolio market value at the end of the interval; V_0 the portfolio market value at the beginning; D the cash distributions; N the number of intervals (monthly); C_i the cash flow (net); R_D the internal rate of return and; r_i the monthly returns.

The investment return is

$$R_p = \frac{V_1 - V_0 + D_1}{V_0}.$$

The arithmetic average rate of return is

$$R_A = \frac{R_{p1} + R_{p2} + ...R_{pn}}{N}.$$

The continuously compounded rate of return affecting the price, P, can be denoted by

$$P_t = P_{t-1}e^{rt} \quad (r = \text{rate of return during t-1,t})$$
$$P_{t_{12}} = P_0e^{r_1+r_2+r_3...+r_{12}} \quad (r_i = \text{returns for month i})$$

Table 8.1. Portfolio risk

outcome	1	2	3	4	5
possible return	50	30	10	-10	-30
probability	0.1	0.2	0.4	0.2	0.1

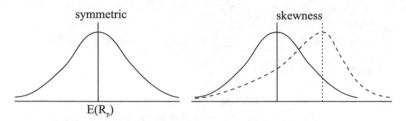

Fig. 8.1. Different types of risk

and the average monthly return is: $r = (r_1 + r_2 ...)/12$

The internal rate of return, R_D, is defined as

$$V_0 = \frac{C_1}{(1 + R_D)} + \frac{C_2}{(1 + R_D)} + \frac{C_N + V_N}{(1 + R_D)^n}$$

Next, let us introduce the portfolio theory. A portfolio of assets (securities) is supposed to maximize the return for the investors for some level of risk they are willing to accept. This is called the Markowitz efficient portfolio. The assumption is that investors are risk adverse. The two fund theory comprises a risk free asset (short term government bonds) and risky assets (stocks).

Let us illustrate a portfolio risk. Take the following data[1]

The expected portfolio return, formally stated, is

$$E(R_p) = P_1 R_1 + P_2 R_2 + ... + P_n R_n$$
$$= \sum_{j=1}^{n} P_j R_j$$

Using the above example we obtain $E(R_p) = 10\%$. Hereby the P_j are the associated probabilities.

Two typical distributions of asset returns are shown in Fig. 8.1.

The variance of the returns is

$$Var(R_p) = P_1(R_1 - E(R_p))^2 + P_2(R_2 - E(R_p))^2 + ...P_n(R_n - E(R_n))^2$$
$$= \sum_{j=1}^{n} P_j(R_j - E(R_p))^2$$

---

[1] The data for the subsequent example is from Fabozzi and Modigliani (1997, Chap. 8).

Table 8.2. Covariance and diversification

Number of Securities in Portfolio	Average Return (%/mo.)	Standard Deviation of Return (%/mo.)	Correlation Coefficient with Market R	Coefficient of Determination with Market R^2
1	0.88	7.0	0.54	0.29
2	0.69	5.0	0.63	0.40
3	0.74	4.8	0.75	0.56
4	0.65	4.6	0.77	0.59
5	0.71	4.6	0.79	0.62
10	0.68	4.2	0.85	0.72
15	0.69	4.0	0.88	0.77
20	0.67	3.9	0.89	0.80

From the above example we have a variance of 480%. This gives a standard deviation $\sigma = \sqrt{480} = 22\%$.

An asset price is said to follow a random walk if the expected future price change is independent of past price changes. Risk for a longer horizon (volatility) is defined as $\sigma \cdot \sqrt{N}$ whereby N are the time periods ahead.

Diversification serves the purpose of constructing a portfolio to reduce portfolio risk without sacrificing return. Diversification does not systematically affect the return of the portfolio. It is equal to the weighted average of individual security returns. Yet, diversification reduces the standard deviation of returns. The standard deviation, σ_p, decreases the less there is a correlation among securities. We define the correlation coefficient as

$$R = \frac{cov(R_i, R_M)}{\sigma_{R_i} \cdot \sigma_M}$$

with the covariance,

$$cov = \frac{1}{N} \sum_t (R_{i_t} - E(R_i))(R_{M_t} - E(R_M)).$$

The example of Table 8.2 shows how risk falls with increasing diversification.[2] In fact the Table 8.2 shows the risk versus diversification for randomly selected portfolios (June 1960–May 1970).

From the above table we can observe the following results. First, the average return is unrelated to the number of securities, second there is a decline in portfolio risk (with the number of securities). Third, there is an increasing correlation with the index of NYSE stocks. Fourth, the R^2, measuring the return of the portfolio with

---

[2]The data of the Table 8.2 is based on the data reported in Fabozzi and Modigliani (1997, Chap. 8).

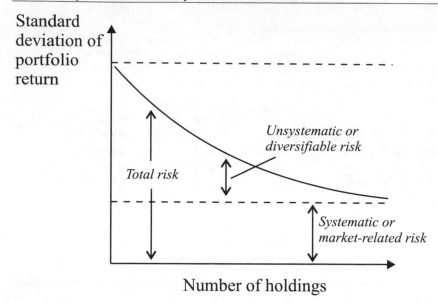

Fig. 8.2. Distribution of asset returns

market return ($0 < R^2 < 1$) rises with the degree of portfolio diversification (a well diversified portfolio has a high R^2). Thus, as Fig. 8.2 indicates, unsystematic risk tends to be diversified with the number of holdings, but systematic risk is not.

Portfolio mean returns are

$$E(R_p) = \gamma_1 E(R_1) + \gamma_2 E(R_2). \tag{8.1}$$

The portfolio variance ($\sigma_{R_p}^2$) for two assets is

$$\sigma_{R_p}^2 = \gamma_1^2 \sigma_{R_1}^2 + \gamma_2^2 \sigma_{R_2}^2 + 2\gamma_1\gamma_2\sigma_{R_1}^2\sigma_{R_2}^2 cov\,(R_1, R_2). \tag{8.2}$$

The portfolio variance is the sum of the weighted variances of the two assets plus the weighted correlation between the two assets.

In general we have

$$\sigma_{R_p}^2 = \sum_{g=1}^{G} \gamma_g^2 \sigma_{R_g}^2 + \sum_{g=1}^{G}\sum_{b=1}^{G} \gamma_g\gamma_b cov(R_g, R_b).$$

Markowitz efficient portfolios are defined by using the mean-variance methodology. This is illustrated by the following. There are two approaches
1) One fund theory refers to risky assets only.
2) Two fund theory refers to risky assets and a risk free asset.

In Fig. 8.3 the capital market line (CML) or the Sharpe Ratio,

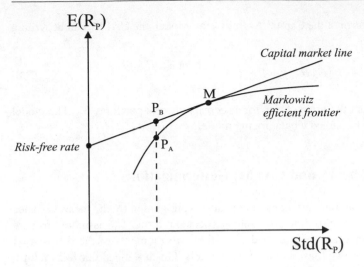

Fig. 8.3. Markowitz efficient frontier

$$SR = \frac{E(R_p) - R_F}{\sigma_p},$$

is an important measure in capital asset pricing. From the Fig. 8.3 we also observe that a portfolio P_B will dominate a portfolio P_A. Yet, we want to note that recent empirical research shows that the Sharpe-ratio and thus the expected equity premium and risk, measured by the standard deviation of the equity premium, are time varying, see Lettau and Ludvigson (2001b). In particular the Sharpe-ratio is moving counter-cyclically, see Wöhrmann, Semmler and Lettau (2001). This, in turn, means that there is a predictable component in the equity premium, since risk is not fully priced in the equity premium.

For the two fund portfolio we can derive

$$E(R_p) = \gamma_F R_F + \gamma_M E(R_M), \ \gamma_F = 1 - \gamma_M \tag{8.3}$$

$$E(R_p) = (1 - \gamma_M) R_F + \gamma_M E(R_m) \tag{8.4}$$

$$E(R_p) = R_F + \gamma_M \left[E(R_M) - R_F \right]. \tag{8.5}$$

Using (8.2) gives (note that R_F carries no risk)

$$\sigma_{R_p}^2 = \gamma_M^2 \sigma_{R_M}^2 \tag{8.6}$$

and

$$\sigma_{R_p} = \gamma_M \sigma_{R_M} \ \Rightarrow \ \gamma_M = \frac{\sigma_{R_p}}{\sigma_{R_M}}. \tag{8.7}$$

Equation (8.5) represents the capital market line and the investor's risk preference would determine a position on this line. A greater γ_M reflects a greater preference for risk.

The standard form of the Capital Asset Pricing Model, the CAPM, can be written as follows

$$E(R_i) = R_F + \beta_i \left[E\left(R_M\right) - R_F \right]; \; \beta_i = \frac{cov(R_i, R_M)}{\sigma^2_{R_M}}. \tag{8.8}$$

The β_i represent the price of risk for a security R_i or a portfolio R_p. The model (8.8) is therefore also called a beta pricing model.

8.3 Portfolio Theory and CAPM: Generalizations

In general if the economic decisions of consumers are guided by the mean-variance methodology they maximize the discounted expected returns. The assumptions here are one, that the investors only consider the first two moments of the distribution of stock returns and two, have homogenous beliefs. Given a mean portfolio return, investors (price takers) choose the one with lowest variance. The investment horizon is one period. There are perfect markets. Investments are infinitely divisible, there are no transaction costs and taxes and there are no short-sale restrictions.

The risk and return trade-off for a portfolio of n assets considers a portfolio P with n assets, weights $\omega' = (\omega_1, \ldots, \omega_n)$ with $\omega' 1 = 1$, 1 a vector of ones, returns $r' = (r_1, \ldots, r_n)$, mean returns μ_r and variance-covariance matrix $\Sigma = \{\sigma_{ij}\}_{i,j=1,\ldots,n}$. The mean of the portfolio return is $\mu_{r_P} = \omega' r$ and the variance $\sigma^2_{R_P} = \omega' V \omega$ with $V = Cov(\sigma)$. The minimum variance portfolios and the efficient frontier is given by

$$\min_{\omega} \omega' V \omega \tag{8.9}$$

$$s.t. \quad \omega' r = \bar{\mu}_{r_P}$$
$$\omega 1 = 1.$$

The mean-variance portfolio produces the efficient frontier as shown in Fig. 8.3. For computing the graph of the efficient frontier in Fig. 8.3 for each mean return $\bar{\mu}_{r_P}$ the minimizing variance is computed and the relationship to the mean return plotted. The computation of the efficient frontier is undertaken with a quadratic programming approach[3], see also Benninga (1998). Further details on the computational aspects of the CAPM, and the multifactor approach arbitrage pricing theory (APT), can be found in Benninga (1998) and Campbell, Lo and MacKinlay (1997, Chaps. 5–6).

The CAPM, according to Black (1972), presumes no risk-free asset. Thus:

$$r_i - r_Z = \beta_i(r_M - r_Z) \quad \text{with} \quad \beta_i = \frac{Cov(r_i, r_M)}{Var(r_M)}.$$

Alternatively Sharpe (1964) and Lintner (1965) do presume the existence of a risk-free asset, $r_Z = r_f$. Their assumptions are that investors are risk-averse, rational, and

---

[3] A Gauss program to solve the above quadratic programming problem is available upon request.

have homogenous expectations. There exists a risk-free asset, perfect markets, and a unique equilibrium.

Then we obtain the capital market line as

$$SR = \frac{E(r_M) - r_f}{\sigma(r_M)}$$

The risk-return relationship is

$$E(r_i) = r_f + \underbrace{[E(r_M) - r_f]}_{\text{market risk}} \underbrace{\frac{Cov(r_i, r_M)}{Var(r_M)}}_{\text{sensitivity} \beta_i} \tag{8.10}$$

whereby the second term on the right hand side of (8.10) represents the risk premium.

A survey of empirical tests of the CAPM are presented in Campbell, Lo and MacKinlay (1997, Chap. 5). For the expected return, $\tilde{r}_i$ and $\tilde{r}_m$, researchers have employed time series regression of the type

$$\tilde{r}_i = r_t + \beta_i(\tilde{r}_m - r_t) \tag{8.11}$$

and the the estimated $\bar{\beta}_i$ regressed on the expected return, $\tilde{r}_i$

$$\tilde{r}_{it} = \alpha_0 + \alpha_1 \bar{\beta}_i. \tag{8.12}$$

Yet, the empirical results are usually very disappointing, see Benninga (1998, Chap. 8). For further empirical studies see also Fabozzi and Modigliani (1997), and Fama and French (1988). The above simple test of the CAPM equs. (8.10)–(8.12) have often failed to confirm the CAPM. The failure of the CAPM has given rise to the development of the multifactor model (MFM) and arbitrage pricing theory (APT).

Advanced tests of the CAPM are undertaken that show that broad stock market indices are no adequate proxies for the market portfolio. Many researchers argue that other assets such as real estate, land and human capital might need to be included in the measure of wealth, Benninga (1998). It is also shown that betas systematically vary over the business cycle. Tests for anomalies and nonlinearities in the beta pricing model can be found in Fama and French (1992). A more fundamental criticism of the CAPM from a dynamic perspective has been presented by Cambell and Vierera (2001).

8.4 Conclusions

So far we have only considered static portfolio theory. Some further extensions and generalizations of the static portfolio theory are given in Campbell, Lo and MacKinlay (1997). The above summary on the CAPM and the brief survey on the empirical work on the CAPM should serve here as an introduction to dynamic portfolio theory. Dynamic portfolio theory builds on the intertemporal framework. This task is pursued in the subsequent two chapters.

Chapter 9
Consumption Based Asset Pricing Models

9.1 Introduction

We here present consumption based dynamic asset market models. These employ an intertemporal framework and thus represent dynamic asset pricing theories. In the subsequent chapter we will study a typical production based asset pricing theory based on the stochastic growth RBC model. Although both types of asset pricing theory employ utility functions, in the consumption based asset pricing theory the dividend stream is frequently exogenously given. However, we want to note that there are other production based asset pricing models that do not use utility theory, see Cochrane (1991, 1996).

Before introducing specific models we need to briefly define the present value of an asset used in this context. Note that the CAPM assumes that investors are concerned with the mean and the variance of the returns. In the consumption based capital asset pricing model (CCAPM) investors are concerned with mean and variance of consumption. Subsequently, the optimal consumption path of a representative household is derived from the first-order condition of an intertemporal maximization problem with a CCAPM model. This gives us the Euler equation and the stochastic discount factor for the dynamic asset pricing model.

9.2 Present Value Approach

First, let us introduce some terms related to the present value approach. A return of an asset is defined as

$$R_{t+1} = \frac{P_{t+1} - P_t + D_{t+1}}{P_t}$$

whereby P_t is the price of the asset at the end of period t, P_{t+1} is its price at period $t + 1$, D_{t+1} the dividend payment at period $t + 1$. The dividend stream may be exogenous or generated through production activities. Subsequently we will explore both possibilities. With a constant discount rate we have

$$P_t = E_t \left(\frac{P_{t+1} + D_{t+1}}{1 + R} \right).$$

The solution by forward iteration of the above formula gives us the efficient market hypothesis.

$$P_t = E_t \underbrace{\left[\sum_{i=1}^{K} \left(\frac{1}{1+R} \right)^i D_{t+i} \right]}_{P_t \,=\, \text{fundamental value}} + E_t \underbrace{\left[\left(\frac{1}{1+R} \right)^K P_{t+K} \right]}_{=\, 0 \text{ for } K \to \infty.}$$

Note that for the efficient market hypothesis to hold the second term in the above formula has to go to zero as time goes to infinity. A special case is the Gordon growth model. Here the dividend is expected to grow at a constant rate G. This model takes account of the fact that the second term goes to zero. For the dividend stream it is assumed

$$E_t(D_{t+i}) = (1+G)E_t(D_{t+i-1})$$
$$= (1+G)^i D_t.$$

Substituting this into the first term of the above equation for the asset price we get, for a constant discount rate,

$$P_t = \frac{E_t(D_{t+1})}{R-G} = \frac{(1+G)D_t}{R-G}.$$

This is the Gordon growth model which shows that the stock price is very sensitive to a change of the discount rate, R. The hypothesis that the expected stock return is constant through time is called the martingale property of stock prices. Of course, the dividend stream will change over time and the empirical realistic assumption is that the dividend stream is persistent in the sense that it follows a strong autoregressive process. For the stock price movement in a production based asset pricing theory, as shown in Chap. 3.6, the cash flows of firms – and the dividend stream as formulated above – result from an optimal investment strategy of the firm and it does not grow at a constant rate, except at some steady state solution. This, at least, would result from a production based dynamic asset pricing theory. Asset pricing for a dynamic consumption based asset pricing theory is studied next. Central to this study is the Euler equation and the different methods to solve it.

9.3 Asset Pricing with a Stochastic Discount Factor

Basic for the consumption based asset pricing model is the utility function of the investor. The utility function captures the fundamental desire for more consumption rather than the intermediate objectives of the mean and the variance of portfolio returns as studied in the previous chapter. The consumption based asset pricing model that we subsequently derive reads as follows[1]

---

[1]For further details, see Cochrane (2001, ch 1).

$$p_t = E_t\left[\beta\frac{u'(c_{t+1})}{u'(c_t)}x_{t+1}\right] \tag{9.1}$$

whereby x_{t+1} is equal to $p_{t+1} + d_{t+1}$, with p_t, p_{t+1} the price of the asset at time period t and $t+1$, β the subjective discount factor, x_{t+1} the pay off and d_{t+1} the dividend.

Take a model with two periods

$$u(c_t, c_{t+1}) = u(c_t) + \beta E_t(u(c_{t+1}))$$

usually one employs a power utility function

$$u(c_t) = \frac{1}{1-\gamma}c_t^{1-\gamma}$$

This is a utility function with constant relative risk aversion, γ. We obtain with $\gamma \to 1$ log utility $u(c) = ln(c)$.

Let ε be the amount of the asset to be chosen and e the endowment

$$\max_{\varepsilon} u(c_t) + E_t[\beta u(c_{t+1})]$$
$$\text{s.t. } c_t = e_t - p_t\varepsilon$$
$$c_{t+1} = e_{t+1} + x_{t+1}\varepsilon$$

Substitute c_t and c_{t+1} into the first equation and take the derivative with respect to ε. This gives

$$u'(c_t)(-p_t) + E[\beta u'(c_{t+1})x_{t+1}] = 0$$

$$p_t u'(c_t) = E[\beta u'(c_{t+1})x_{t+1}] \tag{9.2}$$

from which we obtain Eq. (9.1), the fundamental asset price equation with a stochastic discount factor.

Equation (9.2) represents the loss of utility for one unit of the asset which is equal to the increase in discounted utility from the extra pay off at time period $t + 1$. We thus obtain that the marginal loss is equal to the marginal gain.

Next we show the relation between the stochastic discount factor and the marginal rate of substitution. Let us use

$$p = E(mx)$$

and

$$m_{t+1} = \beta\frac{u'(c_{t+1})}{u'(c_t)}. \tag{9.3}$$

Equation (9.3) is called the stochastic discount factor.

The basic dynamic asset pricing model can then be written

$$p_t = E_t(m_{t+1}x_{t+1}). \tag{9.4}$$

With no uncertainty we get the risk-free rate:

$$p_t = \frac{1}{R^f}x_{t+1}. \tag{9.5}$$

Riskier assets are valued by using a risk-adjusted discount factor

$$p_t^i = \frac{1}{R^i}E(x_{t+1}^i). \tag{9.6}$$

Hereby we denote $R^f = 1 + r^f$, with R^f the risk free rate, $\frac{1}{R^f}$ the discount factor and $\frac{1}{R^i}$ the risk corrected discount factor.

The marginal rate of substitution (or pricing kernel) is

$$m_{t+1}.$$

Thus m_{t+1} is the rate at which the investor is willing to substitute consumption at time $t+1$ for consumption at time t.

The risk-free rate can be derived as follows. We can write from (9.5):

$$R_{t+1} = \frac{x_{t+1}}{p_t}$$

or

$$1 = E(mR)$$

Thus

$$R^f = 1/E(m)$$

and $R = \frac{x}{p}$, since $1 = E(mR^f)$ and more specifically $1 = E(m)R^f$.

For the power utility function and turning off uncertainty, with $u'(c) = c^{-\gamma}$, we get

$$R^f = \frac{1}{\beta}\left(\frac{c_{t+1}}{c_t}\right)^{\gamma}.$$

It follows that $R^f = \frac{1}{E(m)}$, thus

$$R_t^f = \frac{1}{E_t\left[\beta\left(\frac{c_{t+1}}{c_t}\right)^{-\gamma}\right]}.$$

Next we introduce the risk-correction for the equity return. For risky assets we have $1 = E(mR^i)$

We use the following definition

$$cov(m, x) = E(mx) - E(m)E(x). \tag{9.7}$$

From $p = E(mx)$, we obtain then

$$p = E(m)E(x) + cov(m, x).$$

Using the definition of R^f (from (9.5)) we get

$$p = \underbrace{\frac{E(x)}{R^f}} + \underbrace{cov(m, x)} \tag{9.8}$$

present value without risk   risk-adjustment

$$p = \frac{E(x)}{R^f} + \frac{cov[\beta u'(c_{t+1}), x_{t+1}]}{u'(c_t)}. \tag{9.9}$$

In (9.8) an asset whose pay off covaries with the discount factor has its price raised. In (9.9) an asset price is lowered if its pay off covaries positively with consumption. Note that marginal utility $u'(c)$ declines as c rises.

Next we derive the equity premium.
Using $1 = E(mR^i)$ again and (9.7), the covariance decomposition, we have

$$1 = E(m)E(R^i) + cov(m, R^i)$$

and using $R^f \equiv \frac{1}{E(m)}$ we have

$$E(R^i) - R^f = -R^f cov(m, R^i)$$

$$E(R^i) - R^f = -\frac{cov[u'(c_{t+1}), R^i_{t+1}]}{E[u'(c_{t+1})]} \tag{9.10}$$

The Eq. (9.10) represents the equity premium. Here too we can observe that risky assets have an expected return equal to the risk free rate plus a term that represents the adjustment for risk.

Assets whose returns covary positively with consumption make consumption more volatile and thus needs to promise higher expected returns to induce the investors to hold them.

9.4 Derivation of some Euler Equations

9.4.1 Continuous Time Euler Equation

We first derive the Euler equation in the context of a continuous time model. We take a standard intertemporal model.[2] All variables are written in efficiency units,

---

[2]For details, see Flaschel, Franke and Semmler (1997, Chap. 5) and Romer (1996, Chap. 7.)

with c, consumption; n, population growth; μ the exogenous productivity growth; $f(k) = k^\beta$ the production function and γ the coefficient of relative risk aversion. The latter is the inverse of the elasticity of substitution between consumption at different dates.

The optimization problem we consider is

$$\max_c \int_0^\infty e^{-\rho t} \frac{c^{1-\gamma}}{1-\gamma} dt$$

s.t.

$$\dot{k} = f(k) - c - (n + \mu)k.$$

We employ the Hamiltonian

$$H(c, k, \lambda) = u(c) + \lambda(k^\beta - c - (n + \mu)k)$$

and derive the first-order condition

$$\frac{\partial H}{\partial c} = 0 \text{ which gives } c^{-\gamma} = \lambda. \tag{9.11}$$

Taking the time derivatives on both sides of (9.11) we obtain $-\gamma c^{-\gamma-1} \cdot \dot{c} = \dot{\lambda}$. Dividing both sides by λ gives

$$-\gamma \frac{\dot{c}}{c} = \frac{\dot{\lambda}}{\lambda}. \tag{9.12}$$

On the other hand from the derivative of the Hamiltonian with respect to k we obtain

$$\frac{\dot{\lambda}}{\lambda} = (\rho - \beta k^{\beta-1} + n + \mu) \tag{9.13}$$

whereby $\beta k^{\beta-1}$ is the marginal product of capital, which we denote by r. Then (9.12) and (9.13) give us

$$\frac{\dot{c}}{c} = \frac{(\beta k^{\beta-1} - \rho - n - \mu)}{\gamma} = \frac{r - \rho - (n + \mu)}{\gamma}. \tag{9.14}$$

Equation (9.14) describes the optimal consumption path of the representative household obtained in feedback form from the evolution of capital stocks. This is the form the Euler equation takes in the above continuous time model. A survey of empirical tests of such a type of Euler equation based on the power utility function can be found in Campbell et al. (1997, Chap. 8). Next we describe the discrete time counter part for a two period model.

9.4.2 Discrete Time Euler Equation: 2-Period Model

Subsequently, we denote by w_t the wage; $A_t = (1+g)A_{t-1}$ productivity growth and r_{t+1} the return from an asset.

The first and the second period consumption are related by

$$C_{2t+1} = (1 + r_{t+1})(w_t A_t - C_{1t}). \tag{9.15}$$

Then

$$U_t = \frac{C_{1t}^{1-\gamma}}{1-\gamma} + \frac{1}{1+\rho} \frac{C_{2t+1}^{1-\gamma}}{1-\gamma} \tag{9.16}$$

which gives us the two periods' utility.

Then we maximize (9.16) s.t. (9.15) by using the Lagrangian

$$L = \frac{C_{1t}^{1-\gamma}}{1-\gamma} + \frac{1}{1+\rho} \frac{C_{2t+1}^{1-\gamma}}{1-\gamma} + \lambda(A_t w_t - C_{1t} - \frac{1}{1+r_{t+1}} C_{2t+1}).$$

The first-order conditions with respect to C_1, C_2 read

$$C_{1t}^{-\gamma} = \lambda \tag{9.17}$$

$$\frac{1}{1+\rho} C_{2t+1}^{-\gamma} = \frac{\lambda}{1+r_{t+1}}. \tag{9.18}$$

Substituting (9.17) into (9.18) gives:

$$\frac{1}{1+\rho} C_{2t+1}^{-\gamma} = \frac{1}{1+r_{t+1}} C_{1t}^{-\gamma} \qquad \text{or} \tag{9.19}$$

$$1 = \frac{1+r_{t+1}}{1+\rho}\left(\frac{C_{2t+1}}{C_{1t}}\right)^{-\gamma} = (1+r_{t+1})\beta\left(\frac{C_{2t+1}}{C_{1t}}\right)^{-\gamma} = 1 \tag{9.20}$$

whereby $\beta\left(\frac{C_{2t+1}}{C_{1t}}\right)^{-\gamma}$ represents the deterministic form of the discount factor.

From (9.20) we obtain the optimal consumption path

$$\frac{C_{2t+1}}{C_{1t}} = \left(\frac{1+r_{t+1}}{1+\rho}\right)^{1/\gamma}. \tag{9.21}$$

For $r_{t+1} > \rho$ it follows that C_{2t+1} will increase, given $\frac{1}{1+\rho} = \beta$.

9.4.3 Discrete Time Euler Equation: n-Period Model

For an n-period model we have a budget constraint

$$\sum_{t=1}^{T}\left(\frac{1}{1+r_t}\right)^t C_t \leq A_0 + \sum_{t=1}^{T} \frac{1}{(1+r)^t} Y_t. \tag{9.22}$$

Assuming a power utility function:

$$\sum_{t=1}^{T} \frac{1}{(1+\rho)^t} \cdot \frac{C_t^{1-\gamma}}{1-\gamma} \tag{9.23}$$

then from (9.22) and (9.23) we again get

$$\frac{1}{(1+\rho)^t} C_t^{-\gamma} = (1+r) \frac{1}{(1+\rho)^{t+1}} C_{t+1}^{-\gamma}.$$

Thus

$$1 = (1+r)\beta \left(\frac{C_{t+1}}{C_t}\right)^{-\gamma} \tag{9.24}$$

and

$$\frac{C_{t+1}}{C_t} = \left(\frac{1+r}{1+\rho}\right)^{1/\gamma} \tag{9.25}$$

which gives us the optimal consumption path.

9.5 Consumption, Risky Assets and the Euler Equation

Next, we introduce risky assets and discuss the Euler equation for the stochastic case as an example. In the stochastic case the Euler equation reads

$$U'(C_t) = \frac{1}{1+\rho} E_t \left[\left(1 + r_{t+1}^i\right) U'(C_{t+1})\right]. \tag{9.26}$$

The right hand side represents the gain in expected marginal utility from investing the dollar in asset i, selling it at time $t+1$ and consuming the proceeds. We can write

$$1 = E_t \left[\left(1 + r_{t+1}^i\right) \beta \frac{U'(C_{t+1})}{U'(C_t)}\right] \tag{9.27}$$

where $\beta = \frac{1}{1+\rho}$ and $\beta \frac{U'(C_{t+1})}{U'(C_t)} = m_{t+1}$ which is our stochastic discount factor or pricing kernel.

Since the expectation of the product of two variables equals the product of their expectations plus their covariance we can rewrite (9.26) as

$$U'(C_t) = \frac{1}{1+\rho} E \left[1 + r_{t+1}^i\right] E_t \left[U'(C_{t+1})\right] + Cov_t(1 + r_{t+1}^i, U'(C_{t+1})) \tag{9.28}$$

where the latter expression, $Cov_t(1 + r_{t+1}^i, U'(C_{t+1}))$, is as discussed above, a relevant factor in the CCAPM.

For example, with quadratic utility $U(C) = C - \frac{aC^2}{2}$ we have (see Romer, 1996, Chap. 7.5)

$$E_t(1+r^i_{t+1}) = \frac{1}{E_t U'(C_{t+1})} \left[(1 + \rho)\, U'(C_t) + a\, Cov_t(1 + r^i_{t+1}, C_{t+1}) \right]. \quad (9.29)$$

The higher the covariance of an asset's payoff with consumption the higher its expected return must be.

Next let us assume a risk-free asset return. The payoff is certain therefore we have $Cov_t(1 + r^i_{t+1}, C_{t+1}) = 0$ and

$$1 + r^f_{t+1} = \frac{(1 + \rho)\, U'(C_t)}{E_t \left[U'(C_{t+1}) \right]} \quad (9.30)$$

or

$$1 + r^f_{t+1} = 1/E_t(m_{t+1}). \quad (9.31)$$

Next subtracting (9.30) from (9.29) we get the equity premium

$$E_t(r^i_{t+1}) - r^f_{t+1} = \frac{a\, Cov_t(1 + r^i_{t+1}, C_{t+1})}{E_t \left[U'(C_{t+1}) \right]}. \quad (9.32)$$

The (expected) return premium is proportional to the covariance of its return with consumption whereby

$$Cov_t(1 + r^i_{t+1}, C_{t+1}) = \text{consumption } \beta \text{ in CCAPM}.$$

The central prediction of the CAPM is that the premium that assets offer are proportional to their consumption beta.

Table 9.1[3] presents some stylized facts on consumption and asset returns.

From (9.26)–(9.32) one can derive the equity premium in simple terms (see Campbell 1997) using γ, the coefficient of relative risk aversion, be written as

$$E_t \left[r^i_{t+1} - r^f_{t+1} \right] + \frac{\sigma_i^2}{2} = \gamma \sigma_{ic} \quad (9.33)$$

with $\sigma_i^2 =$ variance of asset returns; $\sigma_{ic} =$ covariance of asset returns with consumption growth.

Using the Eq. (9.33) one can discuss the empirical components that might explain the equity premium puzzle. This is shown in the Table 9.2 which summarizes some results from Campbell (1998). Taking the equity premium, the variance of the asset and the covariance of the return with consumption growth, σ_{ic} as given, we see that there is, with some exception, for most countries a very large γ required to explain the equity premium. Here the γ is computed by dividing column 3 by column 5, multiplied by 100. Column 4 is the annualized standard deviation of excess stock returns.[4]

---

[3]The data in the Table 9.1 is based on Campbell (1998) and Campbell et al. (1997).
[4]The data set of Table 9.2 is obtained from Campbell (1998)

Table 9.1. Stylized facts on CCAPM US data: 1947.2–1993.4

mean of real return on stocks	7.2% annual return
mean of riskless rate	3 months T-Bill is 0.7% per year
volatility of real stock returns	annualized standard deviation is 15.8%
volatility of riskless rate	annualized standard deviation of Tbill is 1.8%, most of it due to inflation risk
volatility of real consumption growth	standard deviation of growth rate of real consumption of nondurables is 1.1%
volatility of real dividend growth	volatility at short horizon is 29% annualized, standard deviation with quarterly data, at annual frequency is 7.3%
correlation of real consumption growth and real dividend growth	a weak correlation of 0.05 for quarterly data, at 2–4 year frequency it increases to 0.2
correlation of real consumption growth and real stock return	at quarterly frequency it is 0.21, at 1-year frequency it is 0.34 and declines at longer horizon, covariance 0.0027, $\sigma_{\Delta c} = 0.033$, $\sigma_{R^i} = 0.167$
correlation of real dividend growth and real stock return	a weak correlation of 0.04 at quarterly data, for 1-year horizon it is 0.14, 2-year horizon 0.28

Thus we also can see that γ does not seem to be a very robust parameter and it is, where positive, excessively large.

From the Euler equation (9.27) based on the power utility function one can derive the following testable equation postulated to hold in empirical data for risky assets and consumption growth (Δc)

$$r_{t+1}^i = \mu + \gamma \Delta c_{t+1} + \mu_{t+1} \qquad (9.34)$$

with c the log of consumption. Campbell et al. (1997: 311) report results for US data that are not supportive of Eq. (9.34). Campbell (1998) shows the failure of (9.34) also for international data.

As aforementioned the most common utility function used in economics is the power utility function

$$U(C_t) = \frac{C_t^{1-\gamma}}{1-\gamma} \qquad (9.35)$$

for which the Euler equation is

$$1 = E\left[\left(1 + r_{t+1}^i\right) \beta \left(\frac{C_{t+1}}{C_t}\right)^{-\gamma} \right]. \qquad (9.36)$$

The power utility function is time separable. A non-separable utility function is given by

Table 9.2. The equity premium puzzle in international data

Country	Sample Period	$E_t\left[r^i_{t+1} - r^f_{t+1}\right] + \frac{\sigma_i^2}{2} = \gamma\sigma_{ic}$	σ_i	σ_{ic}	γ
AUL	1970.1–1994.2	3.687	24.080	9.025	40.858
CAN	1970.1–1994.2	2.439	17.209	5.849	41.689
FR	1970.2–1994.2	6.763	23.060	-3.712	< 0
GER	1978.4–1994.2	6.596	21.331	2.480	265.960
ITA	1971.2–1993.2	2.100	28.172	-0.225	< 0
JAP	1970.1–1993.3	7.181	21.689	5.463	131.442
NTH	1977.2–1994.2	9.368	16.189	2.578	363.328
SP	1974.2–1993.2	-0.309	25.668	-0.986	31.310
SWD	1970.1–1994.1	9.537	23.892	0.167	5699.045
SWT	1975.4–1994.2	8.852	18.726	-1.013	< 0
UK	1970.1–1994.2	8.282	22.413	5.500	150.583
USA	1970.1–1993.3	6.245	17.842	3.878	135.255
USA	1947.2–1993.3	7.693	15.597	3.166	243.014
SWD	1919–1992	5.207	18.721	8.385	62.108
UK	1919–1992	8.525	21.802	21.833	39.048
USA	1890–1991	6.211	18.768	30.079	20.650

$$U_t = \left\{ (1-\delta)C_t^{\frac{1-\gamma}{\theta}} + \delta \left(E[U_{t+1}^{1-\gamma}]\right)^{\frac{1}{\theta}} \right\}^{\frac{\theta}{1-\gamma}} \tag{9.37}$$

$$\theta = \frac{1-\gamma}{(1-1/\psi)}.$$

For details of such a function and the derivation of its Euler equation, see Campbell et al. (1997, Chap. 8).

Another non-separable utility function frequently used in economics builds on habit formation

$$U_t = E\left\{ \sum_{j=0}^{\infty} \beta^j \frac{(C_{t+j}/X_{t+j})^{1-\gamma} - 1}{1-\gamma} \right\} \tag{9.38}$$

$$X_t = C_{t-1}^K \text{ or}$$
$$X_t = \bar{C}_{t-1}^K$$

where C_{t-1}^K is the agent's past consumption and $\bar{C}_{t-1}^K$ the aggregate past consumption, see Campbell et al. (1997: 327) for derivation of the Euler equation for those types of utility functions. For a discussion on the use of habit formation to study the equity premium and the time varying Sharpe-ratio, see Wöhrmann, Semmler and Lettau (2001).

9.6 Conclusions

In studying the consumption based dynamic asset pricing theory we have presumed that there is an exogenously given dividend stream which is equal to the consumption stream of the agent whose utility function could take on different forms. For the case of simple utility functions such as the log or power utility, we have also derived the Euler equation as the essential equation to study dynamic asset pricing. Appendix 2 derives the Euler equation from dynamic programming.

Chapter 10
Production Based Asset Pricing Models

10.1 Introduction

Production based asset pricing[1] has been studied on the basis of stochastic growth models. A prototype stochastic growth model is the Real Business Cycle (RBC) Model, which has become one of the standard macroeconomic models. It tries to explain macroeconomic fluctuations as equilibrium reactions of a representative agent economy with complete markets. Many refinements have been introduced since the seminal papers by Kydland and Prescott (1982) and Hansen (1985) improved the model's fit with the data. Often the implications for asset prices are spelled out for RBC models. Asset prices contain valuable information about the intertemporal decision making of economic agents, a mechanism at the heart of the RBC methodology. Here, we summarize results from the work by Lettau, Gong and Semmler (2001) that uses a log-linear variant of the RBC model developed by Campbell (1994) and estimate the parameters of a standard RBC model by taking its asset pricing implications into account.

In fact, modelling asset prices and risk premia in models with production is much more challenging than in exchange economies. Most of the asset pricing literature has followed Lucas (1978) and Mehra and Prescott (1985) in computing asset prices from the consumption based asset pricing models with an exogenous dividend streams. Production economies offer a much richer, and realistic environment. First, in economies with an exogenous dividend stream and no savings consumers are forced to consume their endowment. In economies with production where asset returns and consumption are endogenous consumers can save and hence transfer consumption between periods. Second, in economies with an exogenous dividend stream the aggregate consumption is usually used as a proxy for equity dividends. Empirically, this is not a very sensible modelling choice. Since there is a capital stock in production economies, there is a more realistic modelling of equity dividends is possible.

Christiano and Eichenbaum (1992) use a Generalized Method of Moments (GMM) procedure to estimate the RBC parameters. Their moment restrictions only concern the real variables of the model. Semmler and Gong (1996) estimate the model using a Maximum Likelihood method. The purpose of these sections is to take re-

---

[1]The subsequent part is based on Lettau, Gong and Semmler (2001), for another type of production based asset pricing theory not employing a utility functions, see Cochrane (1991, 1996).

strictions on asset prices implied by the RBC model into account when exploring the parameters of the model. One can introduce asset pricing restrictions step-by-step to clearly demonstrate the effect of each new restriction. As will become clear, the more asset market restrictions are introduced, the more difficult it becomes to empirically match the model with the data. First we report estimations of the model that uses only real variables, as in Christiano and Eichenbaum (1992) and Semmler and Gong (1996). We can report parameters like risk aversion, the discount rate and depreciation. The first additional restriction is the risk-free interest rate. We attempt to match the observed 30-day T-bill rate to the one-period risk-free rate implied by the model. We find that the estimates are fairly close to those obtained without the additional restriction suggesting that the model's prediction of the risk-free rate is broadly consistent with the data.

The second additional asset pricing restriction concerns the risk-return tradeoff implied by the model as measured by the Sharpe-ratio, or the price of risk as discussed in Chap. 8. This variable determines how much expected return agents require per unit of financial risk. Hansen and Jagannathan (1991) and Lettau and Uhlig (1997 a,b) show how the Sharpe-ratio can be used to evaluate the ability of different models to generate high risk premia. Introducing a Sharpe-ratio as a moment restriction to the estimation procedure requires an iterative procedure in order to estimate the risk aversion parameter. More importantly, the model cannot be estimated any more since the parameters become unbounded. In other words, the model cannot fulfill moment restrictions concerning real variables and the Sharpe-ratio simultaneously. The problem is that matching the Sharpe-ratio requires high risk aversion which on the other hand is incompatible with the observed variability of consumption. This tension which is at the heart of the model makes it impossible to estimate. We experiment with various versions of the model, e.g. fixing risk aversion at a high level and then estimating the remaining parameters. Here, too, we are not able to estimate the model while simultaneously generating sensible behavior on the real side of the model as well as obtaining a high Sharpe-ratio.

The theoretical framework of this undertaking is based on Lettau and Uhlig (1997 a,b). He presents closed-form solutions for risk premia of equity and long real bonds, the Sharpe-ratio as well as the risk-free interest rate for the log-linear RBC model of Campbell (1994). These equations can be used as additional moment restrictions in the estimation of the RBC model. The advantage of the log-linear approach is that the closed-form solutions for the financial variables can be directly used in the estimation algorithm. No additional numerical procedure to solve the model is necessary. This reduces the complexity of the estimation substantially.

The estimation technique used here follows the Maximum Likelihood (ML) method in Semmler and Gong (1996). However, the algorithm has to be modified to allow for a simultaneous estimation of the risk aversion parameter and the Sharpe-ratio. For our time series of real variables we employ the data set provided by Christiano (1988).[2]

---

[2]The estimation is conducted through a numerical procedure that allows us to iteratively compute the solution of the decision variables for given parameters and to revise the parameters

Table 10.1. Stylized facts of asset markets: US and European data (unconditional mean and variance)

Variable	US		Europe	
	mean	std.dev.	mean	std.dev
T-bill	0.18	0.86	0.43	0.89
Stock-return	2.17	7.53	1.81	7.37
Equity premium	1.99	7.42	1.38	7.04
Sharpe-ratio	0.27		0.19	

Next we introduce some stylized facts. Then we discuss the log-linearization of the baseline RBC model and the closed-form solutions for the financial variables as computed in Lettau, Gong and Semmler (2001). We present some results for the different variants of our RBC model and interpret our results contrasting the asset market implications of our estimates to the stylized facts of the asset market.

For further literature on asset price implications of the RBC model, see Cooley (1995), Campbell (1994, 1997), Canova and De Nicolo (1995), Danthine et al. (1992), Rouwenhorst (1995), Lettau and Uhlig (1997 a,b) and Wöhrmann, Semmler and Lettau (2001).

10.2 Stylized Facts

Before we report some results of our production based asset pricing models we again want to present some stylized facts that will help the reader to judge the success of the subsequent models.[3]

---

through a numerical optimization procedure so as to maximize the Maximum Likelihood function, see Semmler and Gong (1996).

[3]For the US asset market data represent real returns and are from Lettau, Gong and Semmler (2001), 1947.1–1993.3. All data are at quarterly frequency. Asset market units are percent per quarter. The T-bill rate is the 3 months T-bill rate. For Europe data are taken from Eurostat (1997), all data 1970.1–1993.3, are at quarterly frequency. Asset market units represent real returns and are percent per quarter. The Sharpe-ratio is the mean of equity prices divided by their standard deviation. Following Canova and Nicola (1995) for each of the variables a European variable is obtained by employing a weighted average of the respective variables for Germany, France, Italy and the U.K, where GNP ratios are taken as the weight. This holds also for the 3 months T-bill rate. In the case of the U.K. the T-bill rate was obtained by averaging short term rates.

10.3 The Baseline RBC Model

We use the notation Y_t for output, K_t for capital stock, A_t for technology, N_t for normalized labor input and C_t for consumption. The maximization problem of a representative agent is assumed to take the form

$$\text{Max } E_t \sum_{t=0}^{\infty} \beta^i \left[\frac{C^{1-\gamma}}{1-\gamma} + \theta \log(1 - N_{t+i}) \right], \tag{10.1}$$

$$K_{t+1} = (1 - \delta)K_t + Y_t - C_t, \tag{10.2}$$

with $Y_t = (A_t N_t)^\alpha K_t^{1-\alpha}$, log A: $a_t = \emptyset a_{t-1} + \varepsilon_t$. The latter is a stochastic process for the technology shock.

According to Campbell (1994), from the first order condition of this maximization problem one obtains two decision rules.

The first is the optimal decision of consumption which is of the same type as the one in Chap. 9 where we derived the Euler equation.

$$C_t^{-\gamma} = \beta E_t \left\{ C_{t+1}^{-\gamma} R_{t+1} \right\} \tag{10.3}$$
$$\Rightarrow 1 = E_t \left[m_{t+1} R_{t+1} \right]$$

$$m_{t+1} = \beta \left(\frac{C_{t+1}}{C_t} \right)^{-\gamma} \tag{10.4}$$

the second is the optimal decision of labor input

$$\frac{1}{\theta(1 - N_t)} = \alpha \frac{A_t^\alpha}{C_t} \left(\frac{K_t}{N_t} \right)^\alpha, \tag{10.5}$$

where R_{t+1} is the gross rate of return on investment in capital, which corresponds to the marginal product of capital in production plus undepreciated capital.

$$R_{t+1} \equiv (1 - \alpha) \left(\frac{A_{t+1} N_{t+1}}{K_{t+1}} \right)^\alpha + 1 - \delta. \tag{10.6}$$

At the steady state, technology, consumption, output and capital stock all grow at a common rate G, $G \equiv A_{t+1}/A_t$. Meanwhile, (10.4) becomes

$$G^\gamma = \beta R, \tag{10.7}$$

where R is the steady state of R_{t+1}. Using lower case letters for the corresponding variables in logs, (10.7) can further be written as

$$\gamma g = \log(\beta) + r. \tag{10.8}$$

This indeed defines the relation among g, r, β and γ.

Note that there can be different ways to solve the above dynamic optimization problem. Here, we have used the log-linear approximation method which has also been used in King et al. (1988a, b), Campbell (1994) among others. To apply this method, one first needs to detrend the variables so as to transform them into stationary forms. For a variable X_t the detrended variable x_t is assumed to take the form log $(X_t/\bar{X}_t)$, where $\bar{X}_t$ is the value of X_t on its steady state path. One, therefore, can think of x_t as the variable of zero-mean deviation from the steady state growth path of X_t. The advantage to use this method of detrending is that one can drop the constant terms in the decision rules. Therefore, some structural parameters may not appear in the decision rule and hence one need not estimate them.

Campbell (1994) shows that the solution, using the log-linear approximation method, can be written as

$$c_t = \eta_{ck} k_t + \eta_{ca} a_t, \tag{10.9}$$

$$n_t = \eta_{nk} k_t + \eta_{na} a_t, \tag{10.10}$$

and the law of motion of capital is

$$k_t = \eta_{kk} k_{t-1} + \eta_{ka} a_t, \tag{10.11}$$

where $\eta_{ck}, \eta_{ca}, \eta_{nk}, \eta_{na}, \eta_{kk}$ and η_{ka} are all complicated functions of the parameters $\alpha, \delta, r, g, \gamma$, and $\bar{N}$ ($\bar{N}$ is the steady state value of N_t). We shall remark that the parameters θ, and β do not appear in the different η_{ij} 's ($i, j = c, n, k, a$). Therefore, one can not estimate them if one employs equations (10.9)–(10.11) as the moment restrictions of the estimation. However, one should also note that β can be inferred from (10.8) for given g, γ and r.

10.4 Asset Market Restrictions

Our asset market restrictions attempt to match the aforementioned stylized facts. We thus want to match the following risk-free rate

$$E\left[b_t - r_t^f\right] = 0 \tag{10.12}$$

Sharpe-ratio

$$SR = \gamma \eta_{ca} \sigma_\varepsilon \tag{10.13}$$

Premium on long term bond

$$LTBP = -\gamma^2 \beta \frac{\eta_{ck} \eta_{ka}}{1 - \beta \eta_{kk}} \eta_{ca}^2 \sigma_\varepsilon^2, \tag{10.14}$$

Premium on equity

$$LTEP = \left(\frac{\eta_{dk} \eta_{kk} - \eta_{da} \eta_{kk}}{1 - \beta \eta_{kk}} - \gamma \beta \frac{\eta_{ck} \eta_{kk}}{1 - \beta \eta_{kk}}\right) \gamma \eta_{ca}^2 \sigma_\varepsilon^2. \tag{10.15}$$

Table 10.2. Summary of estimation results

	δ	r	γ	β
variant 1	0.0189	0.0077	1	0.9972
	(0.0144)	(0.0160)		
variant 2	0.0220	0.0041	1	1.0001
	(0.0132)	(0.0144)		
variant 3	0.0344	0.0088	2.0633	1.0015
	(0.0156)	(0.0185)	(0.4719)	

Table 10.3. Asset pricing implications

	SR	σ_c	ξ	LT Bprem	LT Eq Rem
variant 1	0.0065	0.0065	0.66	0.000	-0.082
variant 2	0.0065	0.0065	0.66	-0.042	-0.085
variant 3	0.0180	0.0087	0.66	-0.053	-0.091

Above, r_t^f is regarded to be the risk free interest rate, which is given by

$$r_t^f = \gamma \frac{\eta_{ck}\eta_{kk}}{1 - \eta_{ka}L}\varepsilon_t,$$ (10.16)

where L is the lag operator, ε_t is the i.i.d. innovation, with the standard deviation, of the shock as σ_ε.

In Lettau, Gong and Semmler (2001) we have obtained the following estimation results.

1. Parameter estimates[4]
   Variant 1 is the estimation without (10.12), variant 2 is with (10.12) and variant 3 includes the estimation of γ.
2. Asset market restrictions
   Note that the Sharpe-ratio is SR= $\gamma\sigma_c(\gamma)$ or SR= $\gamma\eta_{ca}\sigma_\varepsilon$. Hereby σ_c is the standard deviation in consumption which can be computed to $\eta_{ca}\sigma_\varepsilon$, and ξ is the leverage ratio (see the appendix of Lettau, Gong and Semmler 2001).
   In contrast to the empirical Sharpe-ratio presented above which is about 0.27, given the parameters from our estimation, the computed Sharpe-ratio is off by a factor of 40 for variant 1 and 2. Due to the slight increase in γ and σ_c, the computed Sharpe-ratio in variant 3 seems to be improved, but is still far away from the empirical Sharpe-ratio of 0.27.

---

[4]The standard errors are in parentheses.

Table 10.4. Matching the Sharpe-ratio

	δ	r	γ
variant 4	1	0	50 (given γ=50)
variant 5	1	1	60 (matching SR)

3. Matching the SR
    We first consider the exercise that $\gamma = 50$ and the remaining parameters, σ and r, are estimated. Note that this variant, called variant 4, is different from variant 2 only in the way that γ is pre-fixed to 50 rather than 1.
    As an alternative exercise, we try to enforce the predicted Sharpe-ratio to be matched to the empirical one of 0.27 when we estimate the structural parameters δ and r. This can be done as follows. First, from (10.13), when SR=0.27, we obtain

    $$\gamma = \frac{0.27}{\eta_{ca}(\gamma)\sigma}. \tag{10.17}$$

    Thus, if we impose the restriction that the Sharpe-ratio of the model should be matched with the empirical Sharpe-ratio there does not exist a γ that would help to match those two Sharpe-ratios.

10.5 Conclusions

We have discussed for the case of a power utility function a dynamic production based asset pricing model and shown that the stochastic growth model of a RBC type with power utility is not able to match asset price restrictions except for the risk-free rate. Boldrin, Christiano and Fisher (2001) take into account habit formation in the utility function and adjustment costs of capital in a two sector model. By doing so they are more successful in replicating financial statistics, such as the equity premium and the Sharpe-ratio in the context of a RBC model but the model then fails along some real dimensions. Recently in numerous contributions further generalizations of the above base line model are considered. This is undertaken in the papers by Den Haan and Marcet (1990), Duffie and McNelis (1997) and Wöhrmann, Semmler and Lettau (2001). In those papers numerical solutions of the Euler equation are explored and in the latter paper time varying asset price characteristics, in particular a time varying Sharpe-ratio, are studied. Finally we want to note that both the consumption and the production based dynamic asset pricing theory have used, by and large, the representative agent framework. Recently, researchers have departed from this approach by employing the framework of heterogenous agents, see Chap. 5.4.

Part V

Foreign Exchange Market, Financial Instability and Economic Activity

Chapter 11
Balance Sheets and Financial Instability

11.1 Introduction

So far we have considered financial markets[1] such as the money and bond markets, the credit market and the stock market separately. Next, we go back to the macroeconometric perspective and consider, more properly, the interaction of those markets, their response to real, monetary and financial shocks as well as their interaction in propagating financial instability affecting output. To study those problems we will heavily rely on the balance sheets of the economic agents. Indeed, balance sheets of economic agents have been at the center of recent studies on the financial interaction, the financial sector and economic activity.[2] We will leave out, in a first step, the foreign exchange market which might in fact be very important for triggering and propagating financial instability. Dynamic models including the foreign exchange market will be developed in Chap. 12. Yet, this chapter will prepare the ground work for the next chapter.

Although the Keynesian oriented strand of financial modelling has emphasized the importance of the financial sector for economic activity, the Keynesian aggregate model has often focused only on money and neglected other financial assets. As Chap. 1 has shown, in the tradition of IS-LM models loans are lumped together with other forms of debt in the bond market, which is automatically cleared when the money market is in equilibrium. In these models money exerts its effect on the real side only through the monetary channel. In particular the balance sheets of the banks, households, firms, the state and the economy as a whole have not sufficiently been paid attention. As we have discussed in Chaps. 3–4, and as recent literature on financial crises has suggested, balance sheets of the economic agents are important in understanding the dynamics of financial crises and recessions. As has recently been maintained, moreover, it is the balance sheets of economic agents, in particular of banks, that are important in understanding the effects of the transmission of monetary and financial shocks to output. In particular monetary policy and exchange rate shocks are transmitted through the balance sheets of banks.

Indeed, a number of recent papers have considered a more detailed transmission propagation. Concentrating on the credit-output relation, one can replace the LM

---

[1]The subsequent part is based on Franke and Semmler (1999).
[2]See Krugman (1999a,b) and Miller and Stiglitz (1999)

curve by a curve which represents credit demand and supply. [3] Then, besides the bond rate, a second rate of interest, the interest rate on loans, has to be introduced. Incorporating the stock market, the credit channel is seen to operate through the impact of shocks on, first, the spread between the loan rate and the bond rate and, second, the equity price as discussed in Chap. 5. This would then be a macromodel with a fully developed financial market, building on the portfolio approach, with a transmission mechanism of real, monetary and financial shocks. Details of such a model can be found in Franke and Semmler (1999).

11.2 The Economy-wide Balance Sheets

Building on the balance sheets of economic agents and the portfolio approach formulates the demand and supply of assets along the lines of Tobin (1969), Tobin and Buiter (1980), Franke and Semmler (1999) and Frankel (1995). Such a version will be briefly sketched here which allows, additionally, for the study of monetary policy and financial shocks. Empirical evidence on such a portfolio approach is provided in Frankel (1996). This portfolio approach which builds on economy-wide balance sheets, can also be used to describe the mechanism of financial destabilization.

Let us assume that firms finance investment both internally, by retaining earnings, and externally, by issuing equities and debt. We disregard commercial paper markets and postulate that credit is solely supplied by financial intermediaries, that is, by commercial banks. The asset side of the balance sheets of firms is composed of the capital stock, which *via* the equity market is evaluated at its equity price, and liquid assets, which are held as deposits in the banking system (possibly to be used for smoothing out revenue fluctuations). Regarding the public, the assets held by private households are equities, treasury bonds, and deposits. The latter might be assumed as non-interest-bearing for simplicity. The government sector sells treasury bonds on the bond market and issues high-powered money to the commercial banks.

The banks hold bank reserves and government bonds and supply loans to firms and banks supply deposits to households and firms. In specifying the demand and supply of these assets, we may also include the perceived bankruptcy risk of firms as an additional variable. This permits us to study the effects of a change in the lending practices of banks that may result from a change in the creditworthiness of their customers. The change of perceived bankruptcy risk usually plays an important role in financial crises and is usually preceded by large domestic or international borrowing. Table 11.1 summarizes the results.

---

[3]See in particular Bernanke and Blinder (1998). Early versions of this line of research are in Brainard and Tobin (1963, 1968), Brainard (1964), Backus *et al.* (1982). More recent views on how monetary or financial shocks affect real activities through the credit market are documented in Friedman (1986), Bernanke (1990), Bernanke and Blinder (1992), Kashyap, Lamont and Stein (1992), Friedman and Kuttner (1992), Kashyap, Stein and Wilcox (1993).

Table 11.1. Economy-wide balance sheets

Assets		Liabilities
	Central Bank	
High-powered money	$M : D_b$	Deposits of commercial banks (interest-free bank reserves)
	Commercial Banks	
Bank reserves	$D_b : D_h$	Deposits from households (interest-free)
Loans to firms	$L : D_f$	Deposits from firms (interest-free)
Government bonds	$B_b :$	CD's
	Firms	
Capital stock (equity price)	$qpK : L$	Loans from commercial banks
Liquid assets (held with commercial banks)	$D_f : p_e E$	Equity
	Households	
Deposits (with commercial banks)	$D_h : V_h$	Total wealth
Government bonds	B_h	
Equity	$p_e E$	

11.3 Households' Holding of Financial Assets

Completing the portfolio approach, we may assume that households hold bonds, deposits and equity. The total wealth of households is, V_h, q represents Tobin's q and p the price of capital goods.

$$V_h = qpK + M + B \qquad\qquad V_h = \text{total wealth.}$$

The asset holding of households is determined by

$$B_h = f_b V_h = f_b(r + \rho, i - \pi, u, \pi, \rho, \dot{\rho})V_h \qquad (11.1)$$
$$D_h = f_d V_h = f_d(r + \rho, i - \pi, u, \pi, \rho, \dot{\rho})V_h \qquad (11.2)$$
$$p_e E = f_e V_h = f_e(r + \rho, i - \pi, u, \pi, \rho, \dot{\rho})V_h. \qquad (11.3)$$

Naturally, the adding-up constraint is

$$f_b + f_d + f_e = 1 \qquad (11.4)$$

where ρ = state of confidence; π = expected inflation rate; r = rate of return on capital and $u = \frac{Y}{K}$, the utilization of capacity.

As the above balance sheets show there are all together four assets: equity, bonds, money and debt. They are assumed to be imperfectly substitutable. Since debt here is inside debt it cancels out. The corresponding market clearing variables are the price for equities, the interest rate on bonds, and the interest rate on loans.

The following signs of the partial derivatives are assumed.

$$f_{br} < 0 \qquad f_{bi} > 0 \qquad f_{bu} \leq 0 \qquad f_{b\pi} \leq 0 \qquad f_{bx} \leq 0$$

$$f_{dr} < 0 \qquad f_{di} < 0 \qquad f_{du} \geq 0 \qquad f_{d\pi} \leq 0 \qquad f_{dx} \leq 0$$

$$f_{er} > 0 \qquad f_{ei} < 0 \qquad f_{eu} \leq 0 \qquad f_{e\pi} \geq 0 \qquad f_{ex} \geq 0, \qquad x = \rho, \dot{\rho}$$

where, with respect to the indices $a = b, d, e$, $f_{ar} = \partial f_a / \partial(r + \rho).f_{ai} = \partial f_a / \partial(i - \pi)$, $f_{au} = \partial d_a / \partial u$, etc. It goes without saying that (11.4) implies $f_{bx} + f_{dx} + f_{ex} = 0(x = r, i, u, \pi, \rho, \dot{\rho})$. The signs state that the three assets are (possibly weak) gross substitutes if this notion is extended to variables other than the direct own rates of return. The only exception is the rate of inflation, which is assumed to impact negatively on money as well as bond holding.

Our model is largely compatible with the recently developed credit view of macroeconomic activity. In a strict sense, the credit view maintains that (owing to the reserve requirement on deposits), monetary policy directly regulates the availability of bank credit (and thus the spending of bank-dependent customers). Taking into account that loans are quasi-contractual commitments then the stock of these is difficult to change quickly, and so we assume that the asset side of the banks has treasury bonds serving as the buffer. In this way banks are able to shield the loans from the impact of tight money by selling off bonds as opposed to contracting credit flows. As bonds are equal to buffers for banks, we highlight this point by employing the hypothesis that loans are actually predetermined in the short run and banks fully satisfy the loan demand by firms. Accordingly, bond holding is conceived of as a residual magnitude in the portfolio decisions of banks.

As indicated above, the stock of loans of firms, L, their liquid assets, D_f, and the number of shares E are treated as predetermined variables. On the basis of equations (11.1)–(11.4) the temporary equilibrium conditions on the four asset markets for equities, bonds, loans and deposits can then be represented as follows (in that order).

$$f_e V_h - p_e E \stackrel{Pe}{=} 0 \tag{11.5}$$

$$f_b V_h + (1 - \mu)(D_f + f_d V_h) - L - B \stackrel{i}{=} 0 \tag{11.6}$$

$$L - f_l(1 - \mu)(D_f + f_d V_h) \stackrel{j}{=} 0 \tag{11.7}$$

$$D_f + f_d V - M/\mu = 0 \tag{11.8}$$

The last equation also takes into account that $M = D_b$ in Table 11.1. In this formulation, the left-hand sides are, of course, the excess demands for the respective assets. The stock-market (11.5) is cleared by variations of the equity price p_e, the bond market (11.6) by the bond rate i, and the loan market (11.7) by the loan rate j. Walras' law applies and equilibrium in these three markets ensures equilibrium on the remaining money market (11.8). As a matter of fact, bond and stock market equilibrium will already be sufficient for this.

Table 11.2. Qualitative impact effects on temporary equilibrium variables

Response in	u	π	ρ	$\dot{\rho}$	α_e	λ	m	b	d
i		+	+	+	-	+	?	?	+	+
j		+	+	+	-	-	+	-	+	+
$j - i$		0	0	0	0	-	+	-	0	0
q		+	-	+	+	+	?	?	?	-

Tobin's q is defined in our context

$$q = (p_e E + L + D_f)/pK \tag{11.9}$$

The following normalization is used

$$b = B/pK, \ d = D_f/pK, \ m = M/pK, \ \lambda = L/pK$$

Though loans are predetermined, full financial equilibrium can still prevail if it is assumed that the loan rate is instantaneously adjusted to that level at which banks just wish to supply this amount of credit. In addition, however, we also consider lagged adjustments of the loan rate, which means that banks are temporarily off their loan supply curve. This modelling device is based on the notion of imperfect competition in the banking sector. In particular, banks have explicit or implicit credit line commitments to firms within the short period which they feel compelled to honour at the going interest rate. Competition then increases (decreases) the loan rate in the next period if the loans presently advanced exceed (fall short of) the amount of credit that banks wish to supply, but this adjustment is only partial.

11.4 Shocks and Financial Market Reactions

Franke and Semmler (1999) undertake a comparative static exercise for the above portfolio approach, based on economy-wide balance sheets as shown in Table 11.1. This gives us information on the financial markets reaction to real, monetary and financial shocks. The Table 11.2 reports qualitative results of those shocks.

Ceteris Paribus, increases in the variables listed in the first row results in the following changes to the bond rate, loan rate, interest spread and stock price.

The notation is: i is the bond rate, j the loan rate, q Tobin's q. At the bond rate i_{EB}, the equity and bond market are clearing while the loan rate is held constant. u denotes the output-capital ratio, π the expected rate of inflation, ρ the public's state of confidence, $\dot{\rho}$ its time derivative, a_e banks' willingness to lend, λ the debt-asset ratio of firms, m the monetary base, b bonds outstanding and, d deposits of firms (the latter three stock variables are also in relation to the capital stock).

Table 11.2 reports interesting results of how shocks are translated into financial market reactions. The question mark represents an ambiguous reaction. Most of the signs in Table 11.2 represent results from our comparative static exercise that one would also expect from a study of empirical data. In particular we want to note that banks' willingness to lend, expressed in α_e, produces the expected signs for the bond rate (rising), loan rate (falling) and equity price (rising). On the other hand, as well known from financial crises, the banks' actions to restrict loans (or recalling loans) – a falling α_e – will give rise, among other things, to rising interest rates and falling stock prices. This is a scenario that we will again find useful in Chap. 12.

11.5 Conclusions

To sum up, we have strived to sketch a model of the financial sector that is, so to speak, ready for use for studying the impact of financial shocks on the real side of the economy (for example in a small macro economic model). A related model that formulates the financial-real interaction in a consistent way can be found in Flaschel, Franke and Semmler (1997, Chap. 12). There, however, the financial market includes only money, credit and stock markets. Leaving out the bond market, the full interaction with the real side, the IS-side of the economy, is then easier to describe and to analyze. There we also show how the financial-real interaction with endogenized Keynesian long swings from the "state of confidence" can give rise to a strong impact on real activity. In the approach presented here fluctuations arise from monetary or financial shocks, propagated through the balance sheets of the economic agents to the real side of the economy. This approach suffices as a framework that will help to explain how external shocks to an economy, for example exchange rate shocks, may generate a financial crisis and large output loss. This is considered next.

Chapter 12
Exchange Rate Volatility and Financial Crisis

12.1 Introduction

This chapter is concerned with exchange rate volatility, balance sheets and the economic activity of economic agents and asset prices. Indeed, with the end of the Bretton Woods system in the 1970s and the financial market liberalization of the 1980s and 1990s, the international economy has experienced several financial crises in certain countries and regions which entailed in most cases, credit contraction, asset price depreciation, declining economic activity and large output losses. This occurred whether the exchange rates were pegged or flexible. There appear to be destabilizing mechanisms at work from which even flexible exchange rate regimes cannot escape. Subsequently, we review some of the stylized facts that appear to be common to such financial crises and survey some recent theories that attempt to model such exchange rate-caused financial and real crises.

With respect to exchange rates and financial and real crises, three views, in fact, three generations of models, have been presented in the literature. A first view maintains that news on macroeconomic fundamentals (differences in economic growth rates, productivity and price levels, short term interest rates as well as monetary policy actions) causes exchange rate movements. The second view maintains that speculative forces e.g., self-fulfilling expectations may be at work, which destabilize exchange rates without deterioration of fundamentals. Third, following the theory of imperfect capital markets, it has also been maintained that the dynamics of self-fulfilling expectations depend on some fundamentals, for example, the strength and weakness of the balance sheets of the economic units such as households, firms, banks and governments. From the latter point of view we can properly study the connection between the deterioration of fundamentals, exchange rate volatility, financial instability and declining economic activity. Although, diverse micro-, as well as macro-economic theories to explain financially caused recessions have been proposed, we think that those models which are particularly relevant are those that exhibit non-linearities and multiple equilibria. Such models appear to be particularly suited to explaining recent financial crises which have caused large output losses.

12.2 Stylized Facts

There have been three major episodes of international financial crisis for certain regions or countries entailing a large output loss. They were 1) the 1980s Latin American debt crisis, 2) the 1994–95 Tequila crisis (Mexico, Argentina), 3) the 1997–98 Asian financial crises (as well as the Russian financial crisis 1998). To study such crises we will look at the interplay of exchange rates, financial markets, the severe reversal of financial flows and large output losses.

Central in this context will be the balance sheets of firms, households, banks and governments. The weak balance sheets of these economic units mean that liabilities are not covered by assets. In particular, heavy external liabilities of economic units such as firms, banks or countries can cause a sudden reversal of capital flows initiating a currency crisis. Exchange rate risk and a sudden reversal of capital flows is often built up by a preceding increase of insolvency risk. The deterioration of balance sheets of households, firms and banks often have come about through a preceding lending boom and an increase in risk taking. A currency crisis is likely to entail a rise in the interest rate, a stock market crash and a banking crisis. Yet, financial and exchange rate volatility does not always lead to an interest rate increase and a stock market crash. It is thus not necessary that financial instability be propagated. The major issue in fact is what the assets of the economic units represent. If economic units borrow against future income streams, they may use net worth as collateral. The wealth of the economic units, or of a country for that matter, are the discounted future income streams. Sufficient net wealth makes agents solvent, otherwise they are threatened by insolvency, which is equivalent to saying that liabilities outweigh assets. The question is only what are good proxies to measure insolvency, i.e. what is sustainable debt?[1] But of course, exchange rate volatility and currency crisis are relevant factors as well and are what determine exchange rate movements.

There are typical stylized facts to be observed before and after the financial crises which have been studied in numerous papers [2]. Empirical literature on financial crisis episodes may allow us to summarize the following stylized facts:[3]

– there is a deterioration of the balance sheets of economic units (households, firms, banks, the government and the country)
– before the crisis the current account deficit to GDP ratio rises
– preceding the currency crisis the external debt to reserve ratio rises (after the crisis the current account recovers)
– there is a sudden reversal of capital flows and unexpected depreciation of the currency
– domestic interest rates jump up (partly initiated by central bank policy)

---

[1]In Chaps. 3.2 a procedure is proposed of how to determine and estimate sustainable debt. A sketch of this model and estimations are undertaken in Chap. 4.4. For debt dynamics in a macro model, see Chiarella et al. (2000, Chap. 3).
[2]See for example Mishkin (1998), Milesi-Ferretti and Razin (1996, 1998).
[3]For a summary of the following stylized facts, see Kamin (1999).

– subsequently stock prices fall
– a banking crisis occurs with large loan losses by banks and subsequent contraction of credit (sometimes moderated by a bail out of failing banks by the government)
– the financial crisis entails a large output loss due to large scale bankruptcies of firms and financial institutions

Since most of the recent financial crises were indeed triggered by a sudden reversal of capital flows and an unexpected depreciation of the currency (partly caused by deteriorating fundamentals, such as the balance sheets of agents, the current account deficit, rising foreign debt and a declining short term debt to reserve ratio) we will first consider the traditional exchange rate model to study whether it helps us to understand the above financial crisis mechanism.

12.3 The Standard Exchange Rate Overshooting Model

In earlier work, starting with Dornbusch's seminal paper on open economy dynamics (1976) and in following contributions by other authors, the economy is stylized in a very simple way through an asset market and a product market. The asset market, represented by the money market, is always at a temporary equilibrium which clears by the fast adjustment of the nominal interest rate. In the product market, prices are postulated to adjust in a Walrasian fashion. In flex-price models the temporary equilibrium in the product market is established through the fast adjustment of prices. Alternatively, it is often assumed that prices are sticky or prices move only sluggishly. In the next section we consider the case when output is fixed and prices move to clear the market. In Sect. 4 we study a model of the IS-type where prices are sticky and output moves.

Dornbusch's original version belongs to the first variant of flexible prices. His model, as well as subsequent papers employ a differential equation approach to formulate the exchange rate and the price dynamics. With the assumption of perfect foresight, the change of the expected exchange rate is then equated with the right hand derivative of the actual exchange rate. This assumption is related to the interest rate parity theory. The same is proposed, where taken up, for the expected price change.

A number of variations of this general approach can be found in the literature. For details of such models and their critical evaluation, see Flaschel, Franke and Semmler (1997).

The dynamics of perfect foresight rational expectations models are characterized by saddle path stability. Small displacements from the equilibrium path will give rise to unstable dynamics. In these models it is then postulated that the variable in question – the exchange rate or price level – will always jump back to the stable path, in more technical terms, to the stable manifold which secures that the transversality condition holds. What the observer would thus see is some jump or overshooting of exchange rates when there is some news concerning fundamentals observed. Due to this overshooting, the exchange rate (or other asset prices, if they are in the model) may fluctuate or even be volatile.

Let us study the basic exchange rate overshooting model more formally. Dornbusch (1976) and Gray and Turnovsky (1979) have provided us with basic models of exchange rate volatility. Here, only simple domestic foreign assets are considered. Moreover, borrowing and lending and the credit markets are left aside as well. There is only domestic and foreign currency.

As mentioned above the traditional exchange rate model results in saddle path stability under perfect foresight using interest parity theory. To explain this model we use the following notation:

i = domestic interest rate; i^* = foreign interest rate; x= expected rate of exchange rate depreciation; e = current exchange rate; M = log of domestic money supply; p = log of price level; Y = log of output

$$i = i^* + x \tag{12.1}$$

$$x = \dot{e} \qquad \text{(perfect foresight)} \tag{12.2}$$

$$M - p = \alpha_1 Y + \alpha_2 i \qquad \alpha_1 > 0, \alpha_2 < 0 \tag{12.3}$$

$$\dot{p} = \rho\left[\beta_0 + (\beta_1 - 1)Y + \beta_2 i + \beta_3(e - p)\right] \tag{12.4}$$

$$0 < \beta_1 < 1; \ \beta_2 < 0; \ \beta_3 > 0, \ \rho > 0.$$

The equilibrium

$$\bar{i} = i^*$$

$$\bar{x} = 0$$

$$\bar{M} - \bar{p} = \alpha_1 Y + \alpha_2 \bar{i}$$

$$\beta_0 + (\beta_1 - 1)Y + \beta_2 \bar{i} + \beta_3(\bar{e} - \bar{p}) = 0.$$

Thus

$$d\bar{p} = d\bar{e} = d\bar{M}$$

We obtain the following dynamics.
From (12.1) and (12.2) we get

$$\dot{e} = i(M, p, Y) - i^* \tag{12.5}$$

and from (12.3) we obtain

$$i(M, p, Y) = \frac{M - p - \alpha_1, Y}{\alpha_2}. \tag{12.6}$$

Therefore, we have, as differential equations, (12.5) and the following (12.7)

$$\dot{p} = \rho\left[\beta_0 + (\beta_1 - 1)Y + \beta_2 i + \beta_3(e - p)\right]. \tag{12.7}$$

Equations (12.5) and (12.7) are our two differential equations which exhibit saddle path stability (for details, see Gray and Turnovsky, 1979).

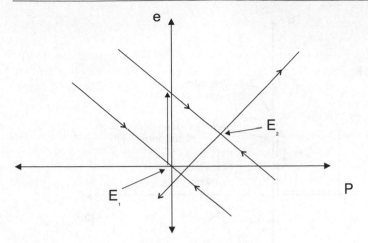

Fig. 12.1. Illustration of the jump variable technique

$$\begin{pmatrix} \dot{e} \\ \dot{p} \end{pmatrix} = \begin{pmatrix} 0 & -1/\alpha_2 \\ \rho\beta_3 & -\rho(\beta_3 + \beta_2/\alpha_2) \end{pmatrix} \begin{pmatrix} e \\ p \end{pmatrix} + \underbrace{\begin{pmatrix} 1/\alpha_2 \\ \rho\beta_2/\alpha_2 \end{pmatrix} m(t)}_{\text{drift term (can be neglected for the local dynamics)}} \quad . \quad (12.8)$$

Here, however, e is free to jump instantaneously to the stable branch of the saddle paths. Thus, the usual jump variable technique is applied.

"This frees e to jump at time zero, thereby rendering the predetermined value e_0 irrelevant for the future evolution of the system" (Gray and Turnovsky, 1979:649) "...we find that an important role in the solution procedure is played by the transversality conditions... The effect of imposing these conditions is typically to force the system on to the stable arm of the saddle, thereby ensuring stability of the resulting dynamic system" (p. 650)

We want to note that first an increase in the money supply makes e jump up and then slowly move down to E_2 (with prices then increasing).

Note also that the product market is in disequilibrium, but the price movement equilibrates it. Yet, we could also assume output changes, if prices are sticky. This is a model to be considered in the next section.

Let us now consider a financial crisis in the context of an open economy with a flexible exchange rate system. We start with the following modification of the overshooting model, again leaving aside other assets and the credit markets.

The financial crisis in the framework of the overshooting model could then look like:

We have posited the following sequence:

1. sudden depreciation of the currency due to an increase of risk (=R), to be included in Eqs. (12.1), (12.2).

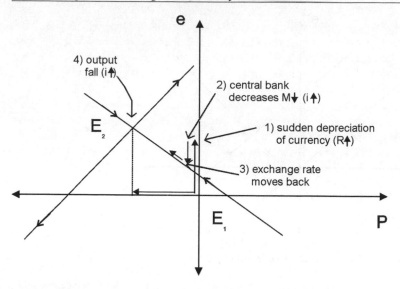

Fig. 12.2. Financial crisis in an overshooting model

2. Central bank decreases the money supply (increase the interest rate).
3. Exchange rate has been overshooting but jumps back to the stable branch and moves to E_2.

Therefore, given equation

$$\dot{p} = \rho\left[\beta_0 + (\beta_1 - 1)Y + \beta_2 i + \beta_3(e - p)\right] \tag{12.9}$$

demand will contract (because i increases) and prices will fall. On the other hand the increase in e has only a small effect on the increase in demand (a depreciation will only slowly increase demand).

Such treatment of exchange rates – through perfect foresight rational expectations models – have been called into question[4]. A variable's jump to the stable manifold requires a lot of information for the agents. Stiglitz has always argued that there are no conceivable market adjustment processes that could allow for such a fast adjustment to the stable branch. In addition, there is an absence of convincing empirical evidence in support of such jumps. In light of these shortcomings, recently economists prefer to employ adaptive learning procedures to explain the convergence to the stable branch. Such mechanisms are then supposed to explain whether and how a rational expectations path is reached. The development of the econometrics of ARMA processes has strongly strengthened this direction of research. Small-scale macro dynamic models in which the right hand derivative of the price level is replaced by one or multi period forecasts of the endogenous variables (i.e. learning mechanism) have already been studied. In Adelzadeh and Semmler (1996) a model is constructed and an econometric

---

[4]See Flaschel, Franke and Semmler (1997).

learning procedure is utilized for the forecast of the exchange rate which avoids the difficulties of the perfect foresight versions of rational expectations models. The procedure does not require the variable under study to be always on the stable manifold (or to get back to it through jumps). The recursive procedure iteratively allows for the adaptive learning of forecasted endogenous variables. One can fruitfully use those learning procedures to understand exchange rate dynamics in open economies.

Yet note that the overshooting model has in place of an IS equation an equation for price dynamics, see Eq. (12.4). In Eq. (12.4) output is fixed. This and the missing asset markets may not be very realistic features of the model and will be relaxed in the next model.

12.4 Exchange Rates, Balance Sheets and Multiple Equilibria

The work by Krugman has been particularly useful in modelling exchange rate volatility, financial instability and financially caused recessions in IS-LM type of models. Krugman has been involved in elaborating on the three generations of models that were mentioned in the introduction.

Recently Krugman (1999a, 1999b) presented some further work and developed extensions of the IS-LM model that include exchange rates, debt dynamics and output dynamics. He has particularly stressed the importance of the balance sheets of economic agents (banks, households, and firms) for macro dynamics. As in Mishkin (1998), with sound balance sheets of banks, firms and households, exchange rate or financial shocks do not translate into deep financially caused recessions. Weak balance sheets are vulnerable to shocks and can be translated into large output losses. This result is obtained in a model of multiple equilibria. Central to the Krugman models is the debt that is denominated in foreign currency as a fraction of total debt. Firms need collateral for borrowing. With low collateral they are likely to receive less credit. When an exchange rate shock occurs the debt denominated in foreign currency rises, the debt service obligation of firms, households and banks rise and – due to the loss of collateral – firms and households receive less credit. Formally the Krugman (1999a, 1999b) model suggests a modification of the traditional IS-model. The traditional IS-model reads

$$Y = D(Y, i) + NX(eP^*/P, Y) \tag{12.10}$$

$$\frac{M}{P} = L(Y, i) \tag{12.11}$$

$$i = i^* \tag{12.12}$$

with NX, net exports, eP^*/P, real exchange rate and (12.12) the arbitrage equation. Figures 12.3 and 12.4 represent the dynamics of the model variants.

The line A-A represents all the points at which, given (12.11), the domestic and foreign interest rates are equal, see Fig. 12.3. For its construction, see Krugman and Obstfeld (2003, Chap. 16)

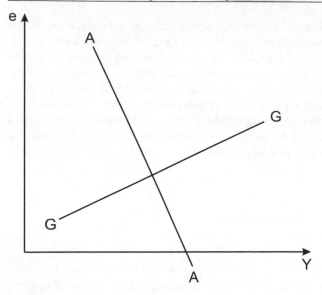

Fig. 12.3. The IS-LM model

The line G-G in Fig. 12.3 shows that output is positively influenced by a rising e (depreciation of currency). The modified IS-model variant with foreign debt reads as follows. With a large fraction of debt (foreign debt) denominated in foreign currency, the net worth effect becomes important with the devaluation of the currency. So we can write (12.10) as

$$Y = D(Y, i, eP^*/P) + NX(eP^*/P, Y) \qquad (12.13)$$

There is a nonlinear feedback effect from exchange rates to net worth and demand. This may give rise to the fact that the economy goes through a low level IS-equilibrium entailing a large output loss. It is thus not a quick convergence to a steady state that makes a financially caused downturn a transitory phenomenon but it is rather the switch from high to low level IS-equilibria that seems to cause a protracted crisis.

Thus, if the economy is close to the middle point of the A-A and G-G curve in Fig. 12.4 (and to the left of A-A), the economy is likely to contract with a sudden depreciation of the currency and a high exposure to debt denominated in foreign currency. The decline of net worth and thus collateral will, through the credit channel, reduce economic activity and lead to low output. For a more elaborate macroeconomic model in which a currency crisis can trigger a large output loss, see Flaschel and Semmler (2002).

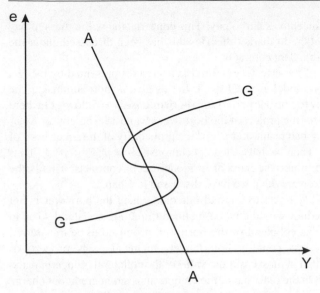

Fig. 12.4. The IS-LM model with multiple equilibria

12.5 Imperfect Capital Markets, Exchange Rates and Multiple Equilibria

Implicit in Krugman's theory is the assumption of imperfect capital markets. The development of the economics of information has made possible the theoretical analysis of credit market imperfections. The main concepts are asymmetric information, moral hazard and adverse selection. Asymmetries of information refers to the borrower-lender relationships. For lenders it is costly to acquire information about the opportunities, characteristics, or actions of borrowers. Financial contracts have to take account of information costs which increases borrowing costs. Risk in credit markets increases the real cost of extending credit. It therefore, reduces the efficiency of the process of matching lenders and potential borrowers. All this may have extensive real effects. The literature on the economics of imperfect information has made an attempt to rationalize several characteristics of credit markets such as the form of financial contract, the existence of financial intermediaries, the form of bankruptcy and the existence of credit rationing and borrowing cost depending on collateral.

Following Jaffee and Stiglitz (1990) we first summarize some elements of the theory of imperfect capital markets. A credit contract involves the relationship between a creditor and a borrower. The first important element in this relationship is asymmetric information. The borrower knows for what purpose the loan will be used, but the lender is less informed about the use of the loan. The borrower promises to pay back the loan with interest. The lender faces heterogenous agents and each borrower's promise is different. The risk of not getting the loan back depends on the borrower's ability to pay back the loan. A risk for the lender may, however, also arise if the borrower has some incentives not to pay. This concerns the willingness to pay by the borrower.[5] In recent credit market theories this has been discussed under the topic of incentive compatible debt contracts.

The essential features of imperfect capital markets are best presented by using a zero horizon or two period model as in Chap. 3. Let us give a short summary. The problem of the ability to pay for the one period zero horizon case is as follows. Let there be two possible outcomes for the project of the borrower x^a and x^b whereby $x^a > x^b$ and $x^a = $ good result; $x^b = $ bad result. Let p^a, p^b the probability of the occurrence of x^a, x^b; with $p^a + p^b = 1$. Then we have the expectations: $x^e = p^a x^a + p^b x^b$. Thus let us describe the second important element in modern debt contracts. This is the limited liability of the borrower which we have discussed in Chap. 3.

Note that limited liability refers to the bad outcome where the borrower is not liable for the loss. The creditor would thus be inclined to require collateral so as to cover any potential loss. The collateral of the borrower, promised to be transferred to the creditor in case of a loss, could be liquid assets, financial assets, property or physical capital. Yet, note that in most cases the value of the collateral is uncertain and may be subject to shocks. On the other hand, the creditor may grant credit but charge different types of borrowers at different interest rate because different borrowers have different idiosyncratic risk characteristics. These interest rates may in particular depend on the size of the collateral that each borrower is willing to offer. So one would expect endogenous credit costs depending on each agent's value of collateral.

A third important element in modern credit markets is rationing of loans that we also have discussed in Chap. 3. Pure rationing of credit might occur only for few borrowers, although all potential borrowers are assumed to be equal. Mostly, credit rationing is connected to the collateral that borrowers can provide. Usually it is assumed that credit is granted up to a certain fraction of the offered collateral.

For the literature on imperfect capital markets and macroeconomic activity, as was shown in Chap. 3, it holds that, although the diverse models in the literature differ in their basic features and predictions, three basic results emerge, providing the basis for the study of macroeconomic financial crises. First, external finance is more expensive than internal finance. The agency cost of lending, possibly depending on the agent's idiosyncratic risk characteristics is the reason for the higher cost of external finance. Second, given the amount of finance required, the premium on external finance depends inversely on the borrower's net worth as collateral. Third, a decrease in the borrower's net worth (value of collateral) causing a rise in the premium on external finance reduces spending and investment of the borrower. This result provides the key to the financial crisis. Since adverse shocks to the economy reduce the net worth of borrowers (or through positive shocks net worth increases), the spending and production effects of the initial shock will be propagated and amplified.

Important recent work on imperfect credit markets and macroeconomics can be found in Kyotaki and Moore (1995). In their basic two period framework entrepreneurs

---

[5]Consider for example the case of a sovereign borrower whose value of the debt is D and M is the value of the access to the capital market. Then if sovereign debt $D > M$ the debtor might not be willing to pay.

operate a technology that uses an input in period 0 to produce output in period 1. There are two types of inputs – a fixed factor K (already in place) and a variable input x_1. The fixed factor could be an input such as land, for example. The variable input could be any kind of input such as raw materials, labor or firm-specific capital. Finally, at the end of period 1, the entrepreneur can sell the fixed factor at the market price, q_1, per unit. The variable input depreciates fully in use and its price is normalized to one. Output in period 1 is $\alpha_1 f(x_1)$, whereby α_1 is a technology parameter and $f(\cdot)$ is increasing and concave. Given the cash flow, $\alpha_0 f(x_0)$, and a debt obligation inherited from the past, $r_0 b_0$, where b_0 is past borrowing and r_0 is the gross real interest rate, the link between the entrepreneur purchases of the variable input x_1 and the borrowing b_1 is given by

$$x_1 = \alpha_0 f(x_0) + b_1 - r_0 b_0 \qquad (12.14)$$

The entrepreneur chooses x_1 and b_1 to maximize period 1 output net of debt repayment. Moreover, there exists an incentive problem, since it is costly for the lender to seize the entrepreneur's output in case of default. In case the borrower does not pay his obligation the ownership of the fixed factor is transferred to the lender. According to the above considerations the fixed factor serves as collateral. With credit rationing the funds provided by the lender will be limited by the discounted market value of the fixed factor:

$$b_1 \leq (q_1/r_1)K \qquad (12.15)$$

where r_1 is the new real interest rate on funds. Thus, there is a collateral-in-advance constraint for spending on the variable input. Unsecured lending is not feasible in this model and thus credit is rationed. By taking together equation (12.14) and (12.15) the incentive constraint is obtained from

$$x_1 \leq \alpha_0 f(x_0) + (q_1/r_1)K - r_0 b_0 \qquad (12.16)$$

where the right hand side of the above equation represents entrepreneur's net worth as collateral. The above equation tells us that spending on the variable input cannot exceed the entrepreneur's net worth. This is equal to the sum of cash flow $\alpha_0 f(x_0)$ and net discounted assets, $(q_1/r_1)K - r_0 b_0$. The constraint (12.16) binds if the entrepreneur's net worth is less than the unconstrained optimal value of x_1.

This simple framework illustrates the results on imperfect capital markets discussed earlier. When the incentive constraint (12.16) binds, the shadow value on an additional unit of internal funds exceeds the gross real interest rate, r_1, prevailing in external capital markets. This difference reflects the agency cost of lending. Moreover, the decrease in the entrepreneur's net worth[6], and thus the fall in the collateral value increases the agency premium, and reduces the borrowers spending (for the intermediate input) and production. The financially caused recession can be explained

---

[6]This decrease may result from a decline in cash flow or a lower value of the collateralizable asset.

by a shock to the borrower's net worth – or the interest rate – leading to a downturn of the real economy and large output loss.

This incentive constraint (12.16) shows the different factors impacting the borrower's net worth, the borrower's spending and the level of production. A decline in cash flow, $\alpha_0 f(x_0)$, a fall in asset prices q_1, a rise in r_1 or an increase in initial debt obligations b_0 reduces net worth. All of them make the constraint binding sooner. Given a binding collateral constraint an increase in r_1 reduces the borrower's spending by a corresponding decrease in asset values, i.e by the borrower's net worth. An increase in the interest rate on previous debt, r_0, also reduces the borrower's spending since it reduces the cash flow net of current interest payments $(\alpha_0 f(x_0) - r_0 b_0)$.[7]

Miller and Stiglitz (1999) follow the approach by Kyotaki and Moore (1995) by including exchange rates and debt denominated in foreign currency in a model of imperfect capital markets. This variation of the model gives then again rise to multiple equilibria. The Miller and Stiglitz paper concentrates on the balance sheet effects arising from an unexpected devaluation of the currency and the impact on highly-leveraged, fully collateralized firms which have borrowed in foreign currency. According to their theory, a fall in the currency triggers margin calls and consequently a "fire-sale" of collateralized assets; the economy may then collapse to a low level equilibrium and a large output loss.

Formally we can write the Miller and Stiglitz model as

$$q_t(k_t - k_{t-1}) + Rb_{t-1} = \alpha k_{t-1} + b_t \tag{12.17}$$

with q, asset price, b, debt, αk, income and $R = 1 + r$. with r the interest rate. From the above we get

$$b_t = (1 + r)b_{t-1} - (\alpha k_{t-1} - q_t(k_t - k_{t-1})). \tag{12.18}$$

With x the loss arising from the unexpected devaluation of the foreign currency loans we have

$$b_t = (1 + r)b_{t-1} - (\alpha k_{t-1} - q_t(k_t - k_{t-1}) - x) \tag{12.19}$$

Without the shock x we have: $b \leq \frac{\alpha k}{r}$. Here again, as in Kyotaki and Moore, the debt should be smaller than discounted present value of the income stream αk serving as collateral.

However, with a shock x we may have: $b > \left(\frac{\alpha k - x}{r}\right)$. The latter case arises from a collateral shock (triggered by unexpected devaluations of the currency) possibly leading to a "fire-sale" of collateralized assets and a fall of q whereby the economy is likely to end up in a low level equilibrium and a large output loss. Note that, here again not all shocks will drive the economy to a low level equilibrium. Only large

---

[7]However, some models have modified the above framework allowing for unsecured lending and the possibility of default. This is the case in models of "costly state verification" where the probability of costly auditing by the lender adds to costs for the borrower. This additional mechanism make unsecured lending feasible although defaults may occur with some positive probability. Some models of this type were discussed in Chap. 3.

shocks accelerated by bad balance sheets will lead to macro-caused financial and real crises. Miller and Stiglitz (1999) estimate the thresholds for those shocks to be a thirty to forty percent unexpected devaluation of the currency to generate such a systemic crisis.

12.6 Exchange Rates, Endogenous Credit Cost and Multiple Equilibria

In the Miller and Stiglitz model the interest rate and the credit cost, per unit of currency borrowed, is fixed. Yet, one of the major issues in modern credit market theory is that credit cost are state dependent. Each agent is likely to face his or her own credit cost. While the main features of the Miller and Stiglitz model are preserved this additional aspect is modelled next.

Credit market imperfections suggest that credit cost is state dependent. In a first view interest rates are perceived indeed as being convex in the agents debt. This has been discussed in Bhandary, Haque and Turnovsky (1995). Work on endogenous credit cost can also be found in Bernanke and Gertler (1989), Bernanke, Gertler and Gilchrist (1998) and Grüne, Semmler and Sieveking (2002). In those models credit cost depends on net worth of the agent (households, firms, countries). Net worth in their conception is the difference between the agent's own assets and his or her liabilities. We follow a similar idea and make the agent's credit cost dependent on assets as well as liabilities (debt). The agent's liability may depend on the debt denominated in foreign currency and thus on the exchange rate. In addition in our model there is an adjustment cost of capital which prevents capital from being costlessly reallocated. Due to those additional assumptions, a credit market model with imperfect capital markets can have multiple equilibria. Thus for income shocks or changes in the credit cost function there can be different domains of attraction and the economy can, due to shocks, move down from a high to a low level equilibria exhibiting a large output loss.

Our model starts from the Miller and Stiglitz (1999) model. In the Miller and Stiglitz case there is a discrete time debt accumulation equation

$$b_t = (1 + r)b_{t-1} - (\alpha k_{t-1} - q_t(k_t - k_{t-1}) - x) \tag{12.20}$$

where b_t is debt, αk_{t-1}, the income, q_t the price of the investment good (in their case land) and $k_t - k_{t-1}$ the investment (land) and $x =$ income loss due to unexpected devaluation of the currency.

In our proposed model there are two changes as compared to Stiglitz and Miller: first, there is endogenous credit cost. Thus we posit a credit cost $H(k, B)$ instead of r, above, and second we take as net income

$$\alpha k_{t-1} - q_t(k_t - k_{t-1}) = f(k, j) = k^\alpha - j - \gamma^\beta k^{-\gamma} \tag{12.21}$$

where $\gamma, \alpha, \beta > 0$. The right hand side of (12.21) represents income generated from a production function minus investment (including an adjustment cost for capital).

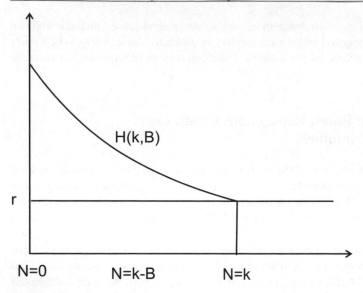

Fig. 12.5. Endogenous credit cost

More specifically, our model reads as follows. We consider a continuous time model and for net income $f_t = \alpha k_{t-1} - q_t(k_t - k_{t-1})$ we take

$$f(k,j) = k^\alpha - j - j^\beta k^{-\gamma} \tag{12.22}$$

with the evolution of capital stock given by

$$\dot{k} = j - \sigma k, \quad k(0) = k. \tag{12.23}$$

With endogenous credit cost $H(k, B)$ we have the evolution of debt

$$\dot{B} = H(k, B) B - f(k, j) \tag{12.24}$$

where $H(k, B)$ is the above mentioned endogenous credit cost. The endogenous credit cost can be defined as

$$H(k, B) = \frac{\alpha_1}{(\alpha_2 + \frac{N}{k})^2} r.$$

Figure 12.5 shows the graph of the credit function where N is net worth.

We define creditworthiness, $B^*(k)$, the maximum amount that the economic agent (household, firm, government or country) can borrow given the initial conditions $k(0) = k_0$, $B(0) = B_0$.

Note that if the interest rate $r = H(k, B)$ is constant, as in the Miller and Stiglitz case, then, as is easy to see, $B^*(k)$ is the present value of the income stream generated by k (subtracting the initial debt $B(0)$):

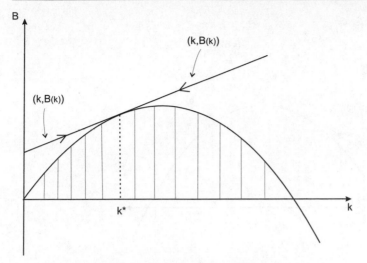

Fig. 12.6. Model with endogenous credit cost and unique equilibrium

$$B^*(k) = \underset{j}{Max} \int_0^\infty e^{-rt} f(k, j)\, dt - B(0) \tag{12.25}$$

s.t.

$$\dot{k} = j - \sigma k, \qquad\qquad k = k(0) \tag{12.26}$$
$$\dot{B} = rB - f(k, j), \; B(0) = B. \tag{12.27}$$

In Semmler and Sieveking (1998, 1999) and Grüne, Semmler and Sieveking (2002) the more general case where r is not a constant is considered. Then, not only the relationship of the present value to creditworthiness but also the notion of present value itself becomes difficult to treat. Note that the endogenous credit cost $H(k, B)$ is determined by creditworthiness $B^*(k)$. Yet, on the other hand, the maximum amount an agent can borrow depends on the credit cost. This is the reason why commonly used present value computations (through the Hamiltonian) are not feasible. Grüne, Semmler and Sieveking (2002) develop a special technique to solve this problem.

Moreover, public debt moves down $B^*(k)$ and exchange rate shocks (depreciation of the currency) decrease net income and possibly increase $H(k, B)$. Due to the assumed nonlinear relationship in the model (nonlinear cost of capital adjustment and the nonlinear credit cost function) there can be multiple steady states. The possibility of a unique steady state is illustrated in Fig. 12.6.

Below the line $(k, B^*(k))$, moving from both sides into the steady state k^*, the agent is creditworthy because the value of debt is lower than the present value from the agent's action. Above that line the agent will be bankrupt.

Figure 12.7 shows the case when there are multiple steady state equilibria. Again, below the dotted line the agent will be solvent and above that line bankruptcy will arise. Note that the slope $(k, B^*(k))$ of the line depends on $H(k, B)$, the credit cost

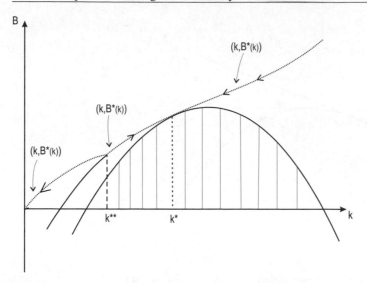

Fig. 12.7. Model with endogenous credit cost and multiple equilibria

function. A large shock to the net income function, a large shock to the exchange rate, an increase to the initial debt, or a change of the credit cost function $H(k, B)$ which makes credit cost rise, will either render the agent – in our case the country – insolvent or make the low level equilibrium (the one with large output loss) an attractor. Numerical examples of those outcomes and further discussions are provided in Semmler and Sieveking (1998) and Grüne, Semmler and Sieveking (2002).

12.7 Conclusions

This chapter studied stylized facts and the basic mechanisms of exchange-rate-caused financial and real crises. As we have shown it is likely to be the connection of weak balance sheets (of households, firms, financial intermediaries, governments and countries) and large exchange rate shocks that lead to positive feedback mechanisms and thus to credit contraction, declining asset prices and economic activity, real crisis and large output loss. This in particular appears to be a basic mechanism if there exists in the country large debt denominated in foreign currency. Moreover, as we have shown, if credit cost is endogenous (state dependent) such destabilizing mechanisms, possibly leading to low level equilibria, are strongly enforced.

Chapter 13
Some Policy Conclusions

The growth of financial markets has exerted its impact on economic activity. The role of financial markets has grown due to deregulation, liberalization of capital accounts in many countries, financial innovations and development of new financial instruments such as financial derivatives. Moreover, since the 1980s, financial liberalization has been actively advocated by international financial institutions such as the IMF and many governments. On the other hand in the last twenty years, almost all countries have experienced major episodes of financial instability, some times with devastating effects on economic activity. This has happened when a fast liberalization of financial markets has led to a currency crisis, sudden reversal of capital flows followed by financial instability and stock market volatility with consequently declining economic activity and large output losses. Of course those developments have also created new opportunities for the financial market traders and investment firms that invested their funds globally.

This book has dealt with financial markets, economic activity and the macroeconomy. An important part of financial markets are the money and bond markets where short and long-term interest rates are determined. We have presented theories and empirical models on the term structure of interest rates. Credit markets, where either commercial papers are traded or where households and firms obtain bank loans, also plays an important role. Bank credit is still the dominant source for financing of real activity (firms, households and countries). Additionally, financial markets contain the stock markets and foreign exchange markets where international capital flows come into play. Economic activity impacted by financial markets was described by the activity of firms, households, banks, governments and countries. In order to study the dynamics of the financial-real interaction we have used micro as well as macro approaches, presumed optimizing and non-optimizing behavior, employed zero horizon and infinite horizon models and have used linear and nonlinear models.

A particularly great concern of ours was the externalities of the financial markets. The experience of financial crises and large output losses in emerging markets in the years 1997–1998 and the large and sudden asset price deflation of advanced market economies during the years 2001–2002 have shown that financial liberalization without proper safety nets, without enforcement of strict accounting standards and government supervision may lead to a failure of financial sectors and have disastrous effects on real activity. To prevent this, it not only requires regulatory institutions and public screening and monitoring but firms and banks need to be required to adhere to strict standards of accounting and publicly reveal information on assets, debt and earnings. Fast liberalization of the financial market entails a greater risk if there is insufficient financial market regulation, inexperienced and loose supervision, no disclosure requirement, no screening and monitoring of financial institutions and no secure safety net for the financial institutions (for example, insurance for bank deposits).

Although implicitly or explicitly discussed throughout the entire book, in Chap. 12 we in particular have demonstrated dynamic mechanisms that help us to explain financial instabilities and financial crises that have occurred in many countries and regions. As we have shown, asset price appreciation through an increased value of collateral, low borrowing costs and wealth effects, can fuel borrowing, lending, and consumption and investment spending. Asset price deflation on the other hand devalues collateral, increases borrowing cost and lets consumption and investment spending decrease. Indeed an interesting feature of the monetary and financial environment in industrial countries over the past decade has been that inflation rates remained relatively stable and low, while asset prices, the prices of equities, bonds, and foreign exchanges, experienced a strong appreciation and depreciation as well as short-term volatility with the liberalization of the financial markets.

There have been, of course, certain regulatory measures enacted for reducing asset price volatility and preventing its adverse impact on the macroeconomy. As remarked above, the improvement of the stability of the financial sector through financial market supervision and banking regulation, such as supervision undertaken by the government and monetary authorities (central banks), appears to be the most important means towards this end. Yet as discussed in Chap. 2, given financial institutions and financial market regulations, an important contribution of central banks might be to not only stabilize output and inflation, but also to stabilize asset prices when they are too volatile.

Stabilizing asset prices, for example, preventing them from depreciating below some level, is not an easy task for monetary authorities. Especially if inflation rates and interest rates are already very low (given the zero bound of the nominal interest rate), it may be impossible. As Japan experienced, in the 1990's, monetary authorities become helpless in stabilizing a further fall of asset prices and output. Central banks, therefore, must, early on, not only respond to forecasted future inflation and output gap but to asset prices as well. Of course estimating asset prices misalignment is at least as difficult as estimating future inflation rates or output gaps, yet one must not forget that future inflation rates or output gaps depend also on future asset prices.

Monetary authorities can and should not target specific levels of asset prices. There are fundamentally justified movements in asset prices as we have shown in Chaps. 2–3 for bond prices and credit cost, Chaps. 5–7 for stock prices and in Chap. 12 for exchange rates. Even asset price misalignments are difficult to measure, as are potential output, future inflation rates and equilibrium interest rates. This should be no reason to ignore them.[1] Monetary authorities should help to provide stability for

---

[1] For a more detailed analysis and for the issues involved see Cecchetti, Genberg, Lipsky and Wadhwani (2002) and Semmler and Zhang (2002).

financial market and reduce the likelihood of financial instability not only in the credit market and banking sector, but also instability arising from extreme changes in asset prices.

Appendices

Appendix 1: Stochastic Processes

An important example of a stochastic process is Brownian motion[2] where dW is the increment in the Wiener process. This is defined as follows

1. linear:

$$dr_t = \mu dt + \sigma dW_t$$

2. growth rates:

$$dr_t = \mu r_t dt + \sigma r_t dW_t$$

3. square root process:

$$dr_t = \mu r_t dt + \sigma r_t^\gamma dW_t$$

   In the latter version the larger the γ the larger is the state dependent volatility. With $\gamma = 1/2$ one obtains the square root process.
4. mean reverting (fixed mean):

$$dr_t = \lambda(\mu - r_t)dt + \sigma r_t dW_t$$

   Note that the mean, μ, could also be time varying.
5. stochastic volatility:

$$dr_t = \mu dt + \sigma_t dW_t$$
$$d\sigma_t = \lambda(\sigma_0 - \sigma_t)dt + \alpha \sigma_t dW_t$$

   The most suitable process to model interest rates is the mean reverting process. For the stock market one often uses the geometric Brownian motion that with multiplicative noise. This also appears in Black and Scholes (1973).
6. geometric Brownian motion for stock prices:

$$dS_t = \mu S_t dt + \sigma S_t dW_t$$

   From 6. we obtain
7. growth rate of stock prices

$$\frac{dS_t}{S_t} = \mu dt + \sigma dW_t$$

   or as integral terms

---

[2]For details of the subsequent stochastic processes, see Chan et al. (1992), see also Neftci (1996), Chap. 11

$$\int_0^t \frac{dS_u}{S_u} = \int_0^t \underbrace{\mu du}_{} + \int_0^t \underbrace{\sigma dW_u}_{}$$

$$\mu t \ + \ \sigma(W_t - W_0)$$

$$W_0 = 0$$

Using 6.

$$S_t = S_0 + \int_0^t \mu S_u du + \int_0^t \sigma S_u dW_u$$

we get 7.

$$\int_0^t \frac{dS_u}{S_u} = \mu t + \sigma W_t$$

(since $W_0 = 0$)

A candidate for an explicit solution of 6. is using Ito's Lemma, see Kloeden, Platen and Schurz (1991), p.70

$$S_t = S_0 e^{\left\{ (\mu - \frac{1}{2}\sigma^2)t + \sigma W_t \right\}}$$

Proof:
Consider the stochastic differential dS_t using Ito's Lemma:

$$dS_t = S_0 e^{\left\{ (\mu - \frac{1}{2}\sigma^2)t + \sigma W_t \right\}} \left[\left(\mu - \frac{1}{2}\sigma^2 \right) dt + \sigma dW_t + \sigma^2 dt \right]$$

The last term on the right corresponds to the second order term in Ito's Lemma. Cancelling similar terms we get

$$dS_t = S_t \left[\mu dt + \sigma dW_t \right]$$

which is 6. If we had not the last term from Ito's Lemma we would have instead from ordinary calculus:

$$dS_t = S_t \left[\left(\mu - \frac{1}{s}\sigma^2 \right) dt + \sigma dW_t \right]$$

which is incorrect.

Appendix 2: Deriving the Euler Equation from Dynamic Programming

Stockey and Lucas (1995) use the dynamic programming approach to derive the Euler equation. Let us write the discrete time Bellman equation as

$$V(k)_{0 \leq y \leq f(k)} = \max \left\{ U \left[f(k) - y \right] + \beta V(y) \right\}$$

where $f(k) - y = C$ and C is consumption.

Using the first-order and envelop conditions

$$U'(f(k_t) - g(k_t)) = \beta V'(g(k_t)) \tag{13.1}$$

$$k_{t+1} = g(k_t); \; k_{t+1} = f(k_t) - C_t; \; k_{t+1} \le f(k_t)$$

$$V'(k_t) = f'(k_t)U'(f(k_t) - g(k_t)). \tag{13.2}$$

Then write:

$$V'(k_{t+1}) = f'(k_{t+1})U'(f(k_{t+1}) - g(k_{t+1})) \tag{13.3}$$

and

$$U'(f(k_{t+1}) - g(k_{t+1})) = U'(C_{t+1}). \tag{13.4}$$

We therefore get from (13.1), (13.3) and (13.4)

$$U'(f(k) - g(k_t)) = \beta f'(k_{t+1})U'(C_{t+1}).$$

Thus

$$1 = \beta f'(k_{t+1}) \frac{U'(C_{t+1})}{U'(C_t)}.$$

The latter is the Euler equation derived from dynamic programming. For a more detailed treatment of how to solve interemporal dynamic optimization problems using dynamic programming, see Grüne and Semmler (2002).

Acknowledgement

The permission by Elsevier Publishers to use data in our Table 9.1. and 9.2 from the Handbook of Macroeconomics, Vol. 1C, J. Campbell "Asset Pricing, Consumption and the Business Cycle" , p. 1248, 1999, is grately acknowledged. We also want to thank Prentice Hall, for allowing us to use some data in our ch. 8 from F. Fabozzi and F. Modigliani "Capital Markets, Institutions and Instruments", ch. 8. 1997.

References

1. Abel, A.B. and O.J. Blanchard (1984) The Present Value of Profits and the Cyclical Movements in Investment. Econometrica **54**(2), 249–273.
2. Adelzadeh, A. and W. Semmler (1996) Fixed and Flexible Exchange Rates. New School University, New York, mimeo.
3. Asada, T. and W. Semmler (1995) Growth and Finance: An Intertemporal Model. Journal of Macroeconomics **17**(4), 623–649.
4. Auerbach, A. (1979) Wealth Maximization and the Cost of Capital. Quarterly Journal of Economics **93**, 433–446.
5. Auerbach, A. (1984) Taxes, Firm Financial Policy and the Cost of Capital: An Empirical Analysis. Journal of Public Economics **23**, 27–57.
6. Backus et al. (1982) A Model of US Financial and Nonfinancial Economic Behavior. Journal of Money, Credit and Banking **12**, 259–293.
7. Balduzzi, A. (1997) The Central Tendency: A Second Factor in Bond Yields. NBER, working paper, no. 6325.
8. Ball, L. (1999) Policy Rulkes for Open Economies. in J. Taylor (ed.), Monetary Policy Rules, Chicago University Press, Chicago.
9. Barro, R.J., N.G. Mankiw and X. Sala-i-Martin (1995) Capital Mobility in Neoclassical Models of Growth. American Economic Review **82**(1), 103–116.
10. Benninga, S. (1998) Financial Modeling. The MIT Press, Cambridge.
11. Bernanke, B. (1983) Non-Monetary Effects of the Financial Crisis in the Propagation of the Great Depression. American Economic Review **73** (June), 257–276.
12. Bernanke, B. (1990) On the Predictive Power of Interest Rates and Interest Rate Spread. NBER working paper 3486.
13. Bernanke, B. and A.S. Blinder (1992) The Federal Funds Rate and the Transmission of Monetary Policy. American Economic Review **82**, 901–921.
14. Bernanke, B. and A.S. Blinder (1998) Credit, Money, and Aggregate Demand. American Economic Review, Papers and Proceedings **78**, 435–439.
15. Bernanke, B. and M. Gertler (1989) Agency Costs, Net Worth and Business Fluctuations. American Economic Review **79**, 14–31.
16. Bernanke, B., and M. Gertler (1994) The Financial Accelerator and the Flight to Quality. Review of Economics and Statistics **78**(1), 1–15.
17. Bernanke, B., Gertler, M. and S. Gilchrist (1998) The Financial Accelerator in a Quantitative Business Cycle Framework. NBER working paper, no. 6455, forthcoming in J. Taylor and M. Woodford (eds), Handbook of Macroeconomics, Amsterdam, North-Holland.
18. Bernanke, B. and M. Gertler (2000) Monetary Policy and Asset Price Volatility. NBER working paper no. 7559.
19. Bhandary, J. S., N. U. Haque and S. J. Turnovsky (1990) Growth, External Debt, and Sovereign Risk in a Small Open Economy. IMF Staff Papers, vol. 37, no. 2 International Monetary Fund.
20. Black, F. (1972) Capital Market Equilibrium with Restricted Borrowing. Journal of Business **45**, 444–455.

21. Black, F. and M. Scholes (1973) The Pricing of Options and Corporate Liabilities. Journal of Political Economy **81**, 637–654.
22. Blanchard, O. (1981) Output, the Stock Market, and Interest Rate. American Economic Review **71**(1), 132–143.
23. Blanchard, O.J. (1983) Debt and Current Account Deficit in Brazil. In: P.A. Armella, R. Dornbusch and M. Obstfeld (eds.) Financial Policies and the World Capital Market: The Problem of Latin American Countries, Chicago: University of Chicago Press: 187–197.
24. Blanchard, O. and S. Fischer (1989) Lectures on Macroeconomics, Cambridge: The MIT Press.
25. Blinder, A.S. (1989) Macroeconomics under Debate. New York: Harvester.
26. Boldrin, M., Christiano, L. and J. Fisher (2001) Habit Persistence, Asset Returns and Business Cycle. American Economic Review **91**(1), 149–167.
27. Boyd, L. and G. Blatt (1988) Investment, Confidence and the Business Cycle. Springer Verlag, Heidelberg and New York.
28. Brainard, W.C. (1964) Financial Intermediaris and a Theory of Monetary Control. Yale Economic Essays **4**, 431–482.
29. Brainard, W.C. and J. Tobin (1968) Pitfalls in Financial Model Building. American Economic Review, Papers and Proceedings **58**, 99–122.
30. Brainard, W.C. and J. Tobin (1963) Financial Intermediaries and the Effectiveness of Monetary Policy. American Economic Review **53**, 71–84.
31. Brock, W.A. and W.D. Dechert Dynamic Ramsey Pricing (1986) International Economic Review **26**(3), 569–591.
32. Brock, W.A. and C. Hommes (1998) Heterogeneous Beliefs and Routes to Chaos in a Simple Asset Pricing Model. Journal of Economic Dynamics and Control **22**, 1235–1274.
33. Bulow, J. and K. Rogoff (1989) Sovereign Debt: Is to Forgive to Forget?. American Economic Review **79**(1), 43–51.
34. Burda, M. and C. Wyplosz (1997) Macroeconomics. Oxford: Oxford University Press.
35. Burnside, C., Eichenbaum, M. and S.Rebelo (1999) Hedging and Financial Fragility in Fixed Exchange Rate Regimes. paper presented at the CEPR Conference on Expectations, Economic Theory and Economic Policy. Perugia, September 1999.
36. Campbell, J.Y. (1994) Inspecting the Mechanism: An Analytical Approach to the Stochastic Growth Model. Journal of Monetary Economics **33**(3). 43–506.
37. Campbell, J.Y. (1998) Asset Prices, Consumption, and the Business Cycle. Harvard University, mimeo.
38. Campbell, J.Y., A. Lo, and A.C. MacKinlay (1997) The Econometrics of Financial Markets, Princeton: Princeton University Press.
39. Campbell, J. Y. and N.G. Mankiw (1989) Consumption, Income, and Interest Rates: Reinterpreting the Time Series Evidence. In: O.J. Blanchard and S. Fischer (eds.) NBER Macroeconomic Annual 1989, Cambridge, MIT-Press, pp. 185–216.
40. Campbell, J.Y. and Shiller, R.J. (1992) Yield Spread and Interest Rate Movements, A Bird's Eye View. Review of Economic and Statistics **58**, 495–514.
41. Campbell, J.Y. and J.H. Cochrane (1999) Explaining the Poor Performance of Consumption-Based Asset Pricing Models. NBER, working paper, no. 7237.
42. Campbell, J.Y. and L.M. Vierera (2001) Strategic Asset Allocation: Portfolio Choice for Long-Term Investors. Clarendon Lectures in Economics, Oxford: Oxford University Press.
43. Canova, F. and G. De Nicolo (1995) Stock Returns and Real Activity: A Strucural Approach. European Economic Review **39**(5), 981–1017.
44. Carlstrom, C.T. and T.S. Fuerst (1997) Agency Cost, Net Worth and Business Fluctuations: A Compatible General Equilibrium Analysis. The American Economic Review, December, 893–910.

45. Cechetti, S.G., H. Genberg, J. Lipsky and S. Wadhwani (2000) Asset Prices and Central Bank Policy. Geneva Reports on the World Economy, no. 2. International Center for Monetary and Banking Studies and Centre for Economic Policy Research.

46. Chan, K.C., G.A. Karolyi, F.A. Longstuff and A.B. Sanders (1992) An Empirical Comparison of Alternative Models of the Short Term Interest Rate. The Journal of Finance **XLVII**(3), July, 1029–1227.

47. Chang, R. and A. Velasco (1999) Liquidity Crises in Emerging Markets: Theory and Policy. NBER working paper 7272, Cambridge.

48. Chiarella, C., W. Semmler and L. Kockesen (1998) The Specification and Estimation of a Nonlinear Model of Real and Stock Market Interaction. mimeo New School University, New York

49. Chiarella, C., W. Semmler and S. Mittnik (1998) Stock Market, Interest Rate and Output: A Model and Empirical Estimations for US and European Time Series Data. mimeo, University of Technology, Sydney.

50. Chiarella, C., P. Flaschel, G. Groh and W. Semmler (2000) Disequilibrium, Growth and Labor Market Dynamics. Heidelberg and New York: Springer Pubibiling House.

51. Chiarella, C. and X.-Z. He (2001) Asset Price and Wealth Dynamics uder Heterogeneous expectations. Research Paper, Institute of Physics Publishing **1**, 1–18.

52. Chiarella, C., P. Flaschel and W. Semmler (2001) Real-Financial Interaction: A Reconsideration of the Blanchard Model with State-of-Market Dependent Reaction Coefficient. working paper, School of Finance and Economics, UTS.

53. Chiarella, C., W. Semmler, S. Mittnik, and P. Zhu (2002) Stock Market, Interest Rate and Output: A Model and estimation for US Time Series Data. Studies of Nonlinear Dynamics and Econometrics. The Berkeley Electronic Press, vol. 6, no. 1.

54. Christiano, L.J. (1988) Why Does Inventory Investment Fluctuates So Much? Journal of Monetary Economics **21**, 247–280.

55. Christiano, L.J. and Eichenbaum, M. (1992) Current Real Business Cycle Theories and Aggregate Labor Market Fluctuation. American Economic Review, June, 431–472.

56. Citibase (1989, 1998) Data Base.

57. Cochrane, J. (1991) Production-Based Asset Pricing and the Link between Stock Returns and Economic Fluctuations. Journal of Finance **46**(1), 209–237.

58. Cochrane, J. (1996) A Cross-Sectional Test of an Investment-Based Asset Pricing Model. Journal of Political Economy **104**(3), 572–621.

59. Cochrane, J. (2001) Asset Pricing. Princeton: Princeton University Press.

60. Cooley, T.F. (ed.) (1995) Frontiers of Business Cycle Research. Princeton: Princeton University Press.

61. Cooley, T.F., Prescott, E. (1995) Economic Growth and Business Cycles. In: Cooley, T. (ed.), Frontiers in Business Cycle Research. Princeton University Press, Princeton.

62. Cox, J.C., J.E. Ingersoll and S.A. Ross (1985) A Theory of the Term Structure of the Interest Rates. Econometrica **53**, 385–407.

63. Danthine, J.-P., J.B.Donaldson and R. Mehra (1992) The Equity Premium and the Allocation of Income Risk. Journal of Economic Dynamics and Control **16**, 509–532.

64. Day, R. and W. Huang (1990) Bulls, Bears and Market Sheeps. Journal of Economic Behavior and Organization **14**(3), 299–329.

65. Day, R.H. and W. Shafer (1985) Keynesian Chaos. Journal of Macroeconomics **7**(3), 277–295.

66. Day, R.H. and T.Y. Lin (1991) A Keynesian Business Cycle. In: Nell, E. and W. Semmler (eds.) Nicholas Kaldor and Mainstream Economics, MacMillan, London, New York.

67. Deaton, A. (1991) Saving and Liquidity Constraints. Econometrica **59**(5), 1221–1249.

68. DeLong, B., A. Shleifer, L. Summers, and K. Waldmann (1990) Positive Feedback Investment Strategies and Destabilizing Rational Speculation. Journal of Finance **45**, 379–395.

69. Den Haan, W. and A. Marcet (1990) Solving the Stochastic Growth Model by Parameterized Expectations. Journal of Business and Economics **8**, 31–34.

70. Diamond, P. and P. Dybvik (1983) Bank Runs, Deposit Insurance and Liquidity. Journal of Political Economy.

71. Dornbusch (1976) Expectations and Exchange Rate Dynamics. Journal of Political Economy **84**, 1161–76.

72. Duffie, D. and J. Pan (1997) An Overview of Value at Risk. Journal of Derivatives **4**(3). 7–49.

73. Duffie, D. and P. McNelis (1997) Approximating and Simulating the Stochastic Growth Model. University of Pittsburgh, mimeo.

74. Dupor, W. (2001) Nominal Prices versus Asset Price Stabilizations. mimeo, University of Pennsylvenia.

75. Eaton, J. and R. Fernandez (1995) Sovereign Debt. National Bureau of Economic Research working paper series, no. 5131.

76. Eckstein, O., E. Green and A.Sinai (1974) The Data Resources Model: Uses, Structure and Analysis of the US Economy. International Economic Review **15**(3), 595–615.

77. Eckstein., O. and A. Sinai (1986) The Mechanisms of the Business Cycle in the Postwar Era. In: R. Gordon (ed.) The American Business Cycle, Chicago: University of Chicago Press.

78. Edwards, S. (1999) On Crisis Prevention: Lessons From Mexico and East Asia. NBER, working paper, no. 7233.

79. Edwards, S. and M.A. Savastano (1999) Exchange Rates in Emerging Economies: What Do We Know? What Do We Need To Know?. NBER, working paper, no. 7228.

80. Estrella, A. and G. Hardouvelis (1991) The Term Structure as a Predictor of Real Economic Activity. Journal of Finance, 46: 555-576.

81. Estrella, A. and F.S. Mishkin (1997) The Predictive Power of the Term Structure of Interest Rates in Europe and the United States. European Economic Review **41**(7) July.

82. Eurostat, Data set. (1997)

83. Fabozzi, F. and F. Modigliani (1997) Capital Markets, Institutions and Instruments. Englewood Ciffs: Prentice Hall, New Jersey.

84. Fair, R. (1984) Specification, Estimation and Macroeconomic Models. Cambridge: Harvard University Press.

85. Fama, E.F. (1990) Returns and Real Activity. Journal of Finance **45**(4), 1089–1107.

86. Fama, E.F. (1984) The Information in the Term Structure. Journal of Financial Economics **13**, 509–528.

87. Fama, E.F. and Bliss, R.R. (1987) The Information in Long Maturity Forward Rates. American Economic Review **77**, 680–692.

88. Fama, E.F. and K.R. French (1988) Dividend Yields and Expected Stock Returns. Journal of Financial Economics **22**, 3–25.

89. Fama, E. and K. R. French (1989) Business Conditions and Expected Returns on Stocks and Bonds. Journal of Financial Economics, 25, 23-49.

90. Fazzari, S., R. G. Hubbard, and B. C. Petersen (1988) Financing Constraints and Corporate Investment. Brookings Papers of Economic Activity **1**, 141–195.

91. Flaschel, P. and W. Semmler (2002) Currency Crisis, Financial Crisis and Large Output Loss. Working paper, CEM, University of Bielefeld.

92. Flaschel, P., Franke, R. and W. Semmler (1997) Dynamic Macroeconomics. Instability, Fluctuations, and Growth in Monetary Economies. MIT-Press, Cambridge, Mass.

93. Flaschel, P., W. Semmler and G. Gong (2001) A Keynesian Econometric Framework for Studying Monetary Policy Rules. Journal of Economic Behavior and Organization **46**, 101–136.

94. Flood and Garber (1980) Market Fundamentals versus Price Level Bubbles; Journal of Political Economy **88**, 745–770.

95. Flow of Funds Accounts (1989) Federal Reserve Bank, Washington, D.C.

96. Foley, D. (1987) Liquidity-Profit Rate Cycles in a Capitalist Economy. Journal of Economic Behavior and Organization **8**(3), Sept., 363–376.

97. Franke, R. and W. Semmler (1997) The Financial-Real Interaction and Investment in the Business Cycle. In: G. Deleplace and E. Nell (eds.) Money in Motion, London: MacMillan.
98. Franke, R. and R. Sethi (1998) Cautious Trend-Seeking and Complex Asset Price Dynamics. Research in Economics **52**, 61–79.
99. Franke, R. and W. Semmler (1999) Bond Rate, Loan Rate and Tobin's q in a Temporary Equilibrium Model of the Financial Sector. Metroeconomica, International Review of Economics **50**(3), 351–385.
100. Frankel, J. (1995) Financial Market and Monetary Policy. Cambridge: MIT Press
101. Friedman, B. M. (1983) The Roles of Money and Credit in Macroeconomic Activities. In: J. Tobin (ed.) Macroeconomics, Prices and Quantities, The Brookings Institution, Washington, DC.
102. Friedman, B. M. (1986) Money, Credit and Interest Rate. In: Gordon, R.J. (ed.) The American Business Cycle: Continuity and Change, University of Chicago Press, Chicago, Il.
103. Friedman, B.M. and K.N. Kuttner (1992) Money, Income, Prices, and Interest Rates. American Economic Review **82**, 472–492.
104. Gertler, M. and S. Gilchrist (1994) Monetary Policy, Business Cycles and the Behavior of Small Manufacturing Firms. Quarterly Journal of Economics **109**, 309–340.
105. Gertler, M., R.G. Hubbard and A. Kashyap (1991) Interest Rate Spread, Credit Constraints and Investment. In: R.G. Hubbard, ed., Financial Markets and Financial Crises, Chicago: Chicago University Press.
106. Granger, C.W.J. and T. Teräsvirta (1993) Modeling Nonlinear Economic Relationships. Oxford: Oxford University Press.
107. Granger, C.W.J., T. Teräsvirta and H.M. Anderson (1993) Modeling Nonlinearity over the Business Cycle. In: Stock, J.H. and M.W. Watson (eds.) New Research on Business Cycles, Indicators and Forecasting, Chicago: Chicago University Press.
108. Gray, J. and S. Turnovsky (1979) Exchange Rates. International Economic Review **20**(3).
109. Greenwald, B. and J. E. Stiglitz (1986) Imperfect Information, Finance Constraints, and Business Fluctuations. In: M. Kohn and S.C. Tsiang (eds.) Finance Constraints, Expectations, and Macroeconomics, Oxford: Clarendon Press, pp 103–140.
110. Greenwald, B. and J. E. Stiglitz (1986) Imperfect Information, Finance Constraints, and Business Fluctuations. In: M. Kohn and S.C. Tsiang (eds.) Finance Constraints, Expectations, and Macroeconomics, Oxford: Clarendon Press, pp 103–140.
111. Greenwald, B. and J. Stiglitz (1993) Financial Markets, Imperfections and Business Cycles. Quarterly Journal of Economics **108**, 77–114.
112. Greenwood and Jovanovic, B. (1999) The Information Technology Revolution and the Stock Market. American Economic Review, 89, May.
113. Greiner, A. and W. Semmler (1999): An Inquiry into the Sustainability of German Fiscal Policy: Some Time-Series Tests. Public Finance Review **27**(2), March, 220–236.
114. Grüne, L. and W. Semmler (2002) Using Dynamic Programming to Solve Dynamic Optimization Problems in Economics. CEM, Bielefeld University, working paper.
115. Grüne, L., W. Semmler and M. Sieveking (2002) Thresholds in a Credit Market Model with Multiple Equilibria. Forthcoming Economic Theory.
116. Hamilton, J.D. (1989) Time Series Analysis. Princeton: Princeton University Press.
117. Hamilton, J.D. and Flaven, M. (1986) On the Limitations of Government Borrowing: A Framework for Empirical Testing. American Economic Review **76**(4), 808–819.
118. Hamilton J. D. and G. Lin (1996) Stock Market Volatility and Business Cycles. Journal of Applied Econometrics **11**, 573–593.
119. Hansen, G.H. (1985) Indivisible Labor and Business Cycle. Journal of Monetary Economics **16**, 309–327.
120. Hansen, L. and J. Jagannathan (1991) Restrictions on Intertemporal Marginal Rates of Substitutions implied by Asset Returns. Journal of Political Economy **99**, 225–262.

121. Hobijn, B. and B. Jovanovic (1999) The Information Technology Revolution and the Stock Market: Preliminary Evidence. working paper N.Y. University.
122. Hsiao, C. and W. Semmler (1999) Comparing Continuous and Discrete Time Estimations with Application to the Term Structure of the interest rate. University of Bielefeld, mimeo.
123. Hubbard, R.G. and K. L. Judd (1986) Liquidity Constraints, Fiscal Policy, and Consumption. Brookings Papers on Economic Activity, 1, 1–50.
124. Ireland, P.N. (1999) Expectations, Credibility, and Time-Consistent Monetary Policy. NBER working paper, no. 7234.
125. Jaffee, D. and J. Stiglitz (1990) Credit Rationing. In: B.M. Friedman and F.H. Hahn (eds.) Handbook of Monetary Economics, Vol. II. Elsevier Science Publishers, B.V., pp. 837–888.
126. Jovanovic, B. and G. Macdonald (1994) The Life-Cycle of a Competitive Industry. Journal of Political Economy 102(2).
127. Kalecki, M. (1937a) The Principle of Increasing Risk. Economica, November, 441–447.
128. Kalecki, M. (1937b) A Theory of the Business Cycle. Review of Economic Studies, February, 77-97
129. Kashyap, A.K., O.A. Lamont and J.C. Stein (1992) Credit Conditions and Cyclical Behavior of Inventories: A Case Study of the 1981–1982 Recession. University of Chicago, mimeo.
130. Kashyap, A.K., J.C. Stein and D.W. Wilcox (1993) Monetary Policy and Credit Conditions: Evidence from the Composition of External Finance. American Economic Review 83, 78–99.
131. Kamin, S.B. (1999) The Current International Financial Crisis: How Much is New?. Journal of International Money and Finance 18, 501–514.
132. Kent, C. and P. Lowe (1997) Asset-Price Bubbles and Monetary Policy. mimeo, Research Bank of Australia.
133. Keynes, J.M. (1936) General Theory of Money, Interest and Employment. London: MacMillan.
134. Kho, B.-C. and R.M. Stulz (1999) Banks, the IMF, and the Asian Crisis. NBER, working paper, no. 7361.
135. King, R.G., C.I. Plosser and S.T. Rebelo (1988a) Production, Growth and Business Cycles I: The Basic Neoclassical Model. Journal of Monetary Economics 21, 195–232.
136. King, R.G., C.I. Plosser and S.T. Rebelo (1988b) Production, Growth and Business Cycles II: New Directions. Journal of Monetary Economics 21: 309–341.
137. Kloeden, P.E, E. Platen and H. Schurz (1991) Numerical Solutions of SNDE through Computer Experiments, Heidelberg and New York: Springer Verlag.
138. Kockesen, L. and W. Semmler (1998) Testing the Financial Accelerator Using Nonlinear Time Series Methods. CEM, University of Bielefeld, working paper.
139. Krugman, P. (1999a) Balance Sheets, the Transfer Problem and Financial Crises. MIT, mimeo.
140. Krugman, P. (1999b) Comments on the Transfer Problem. MIT, mimeo.
141. Krugman, P. and M. Obstfeld (2003) International Economics, Theory and Policy. Boston, Addison-Wesley.
142. Kydland, F. and E. Prescott (1982) Time to Build and Aggregate Fluctuations. Econometrica 50(6), 1345–1371.
143. Kyotaki, N. and J. Moore (1995) Credit Cycles. Journal of Political Economy 105, April, 211–248.
144. Lane, P. and G.M. Milesi-Ferretti (1999) The External Wealth of Nations. Measures of Foreign Assets and Liabilities for Industrial and Developing Countries. IMF, mimeo.
145. Leijonhuvud, A. (1973) Effective Demand Failures. Swedish Journal of Economics 75, 28–48.
146. Lettau, M. and H. Uhlig (1997a) Asset Prices and Business Cycles. CEPR working paper, Tilburg University.

147. Lettau, M. and H. Uhlig (1997b) Preferences, Consumption Smoothing and Risk Premia. CEPR working paper, Tilburg University.
148. Lettau, M. and S. Ludvigson (2001a) Consumption, Aggregatee Wealth and Expected Stock Returns. Journal of Finance **54**(3), 815–849.
149. Lettau, M. and S. Ludvigson (2001b) Measuring and Modeling Variation in the Risk-Return. New York University, mimeo.
150. Lettau, M. and S. Ludvigson (2002) Time Varying Risk Premia and the Cost of Capital: An Alternative Implication of the Q Theory of Investment. Journal of Monetary Economics **49**, 31–66.
151. Lettau, M., Gong, G. and W. Semmler (2001) Statistical Estimation and Moment Evaluation of a Stochastic Growth Model with Asset Market Restrictions. Journal of Economic Behavior and Organization **44**, 85–103.
152. Levy, M., H. Levy and S. Solomon (1995) Microscopic Simulation of the Stock Market: The Effect of Microscopic. J. Physique I **5**, 1087–1107 Diversity.
153. Lintner (1965) Valuation of Risky Assets and the Selection of Risky Investment in Stock Portfolios and Capital Budget. Review of Economics and Statistics **47**, 13–37.
154. Lucas, R. (1978) Asset Prices in an Exchange Economy. Econometrica **46**, 1429–1446.
155. Mankiw, B.G. (1996) The Term Structure of Interest Rates Revisited. Brooking Papers of Economic Activity **1**, 61–96.
156. Markowitz, H.M. (1952) Portfolio Selection. Journal of Finance **7**, 77–91.
157. Mayer, C. (1989) Financial Systems, Corporate Finance, and Economic Development. paper presented at the NBER conference, Boston, 1989.
158. Mayer, C. (1991) International Comparison of Financial Structures. In: Gertler et al. (1991).
159. Mazzucato, M. and W. Semmler (1999) Market Share Instability and Stock Price Volatility during the Industry Life-Cycle: The US Automobile Industry. Journal of Evolutionary Economics **9**(1), 67–96.
160. Mazzucato, M. and W. Semmler (2002) The Determinants of Stock Price Volatility: An Industry Study. Nonlinear Dynamics, Psychology, and Life Sciences **6**(2), 197–216.
161. McMillin, W. D. and G. S. Laumas (1988) The Impact of Anticipated and Unanticipated Policy Actions on the Stock Market. Applied Economics **20**, 377–384.
162. Mehra, R. and E. C. Prescott (1985) The Equity Premium Puzzle. Journal of Monetary Economics **15**, 145–161.
163. Meng, Q. and A. Velasco (1999) Can Capital Mobility Be Destabilizing?. NBER, working paper, nc. 7263.
164. Milesi-Ferretti, G.M. and A. Razin (1996) Current Account Sustainability: Selected East Asian and Latin American Experiences. NBER working paper no. 5791.
165. Milesi-Ferretti, G.M. and A. Razin (1997) Sharp Reduction in Current Account Deficits: An Empirical Analysis. NBER working paper no. 6310.
166. Milesi-Ferretti, G.M. and A. Razin (1998) Sharp Reduction in Curent Account Deficits: An Empirical Analysis. NBER working paper no. 6310.
167. Miller, M. and J. Stiglitz (1999) Bankruptcy Protection against Macroeconomic Shocks. The World Bank, mimeo.
168. Minsky, H. P. (1975), John Maynard Keynes, Columbia New York University Press.
169. Minsky, H.P. (1982) Can it Happen again?. Armonk: ME Sharpe.
170. Minsky, H.P. (1986) Stabilizing an unstable Economy. New Haven: Yale University Press.
171. Mishkin, F.S. (1990) Asymmetric Information and Financial Crises: A Historical Perspective. In: R.G. Hubbard (ed.) Financial Markets and Financial Crises Chicago: University of Chicago Press.
172. Mishkin, F. S. (1995) The Economics of Money, Banking and Financial Markets, New York: Harper and Collins
173. Mishkin, F.S. (1998) International Capital Movement,Financial Volatility and Financial Instability. NBER working paper, no. 6390.

174. Modigliani, F. and J. Miller (1958) The Cost of Capital, Corporate Finance and the Theory of Investment. The American Economic Review **52**, 261–297.
175. Myers, S. (1984) The Capital Structure Puzzle. The Journal of Financial Economics **5**, 147–175.
176. Neftci, S. (1996) Introduction to Financial Mathematics. New York: Academic Press.
177. Obstfeld, M. and K. Rogoff (1999) New Directions for Stochastic Open Economy Models. NBER, working paper, no. 7313.
178. OECD Data-base (1999)
179. Ozaki, T. (1986) Local Gaussian Modeling of Stochastic Dynamical Systems. In: Hannan, E.J., P.R. Krishnaiah and M.M. Rao (eds.) Handbook of Statistics, vol. 5, North-Holland, Elsevier Science Publishers B.V.
180. Ozaki, T. (1989) Statistical Identification of Nonlinear Dynamics in Macroeconomic Using Nonlinear Time Series Models. In: P. Hackl (ed.) Statistical Analysis and Forecasting of Economic Structural Change, Springer Verlag, pp. 345–365.
181. Ozaki, T. (1994) The Local Linearization Filter with Application to Non-linear System Identification. In: H. Bozdogan (ed.) Proceedings of the First US/Japan Conference on the Frontiers of Statistical Modeling: An Informational Approach, Boston, Kluwer Academic Publishers: pp. 217–240.
182. Phelps, E. and G. Zoega (2000) Prosperity and Depression Productivity Expectations and Asset Valuations in Structural Booms. Paper presented at the 31st Panel Meeting, Economic Policy, CEPR, Lisboa, April 2000.
183. Plosser, C. and G. Rouwenhorst (1994) International Term Structure and Real Economic Growth. Journal of Monetary Economics **33**, 133–155.
184. Poterba, J. and L. Summers (1988) Mean Reversion in Stock Prices. Journal of Financial Economics, 22, 27-59.
185. Potter, S.M. (1993) A Nonlinear Approach to US GNP. mimeo, University of Wisconsin-Madison, Department of Economics.
186. Rogoff, K. (1999) International Institutions for Reducing Global Financial Instability. NBER working paper 7265, Cambridge.
187. Romer, D. (1996) Advanced Macroeconomics. London: MacGraw Hill.
188. Rothman, P. (1999) Nonlinear Time Series Analysis of Economic and Financial Data. (ed.) Kluwer Academic Publishers, Boston, Dordrecht, London.
189. Rouwenhorst, G. K. (1995) Asset Pricing Implications of Equilibrium Business Cycle Models. In: T. F. Cooley (ed.) Frontiers of Business Cycle Research, Princeton: Princeton University Press.
190. Schwert, G. W. (1989) Why Does Stock Market Volatility Change over Time?. Journal of Finance **44**(5), 1115–1153.
191. Schwert, G.W., (1990) Stock Returns and Real Activity: A Century of Evidence. Journal of Finance **45**(4), 1237–1257.
192. Semmler, W. (1989) (ed.) Financial Dynamics and Business Cycles. Armonk: M.E. Sharpe.
193. Semmler, W. (1987) A Macroeconomic Limit Cycle with Financial Perturbations. Journal of Economic Organization and Behavior **8**, 469–495.
194. Semmler, W. (1994), (ed.), Business Cycles: Theory and Empirical Methods, Kluwer Academic Publishers, Boston, Dordrecht, London.
195. Semmler, W. (1994) Information, Innovation and Diffusion of Technologies. Journal of Evolutionary Economics **4**, 45–58.
196. Semmler, W. and G. Gong (1996) Estimating Parameters of Real Business Cycle Models. Journal of Economic Behavior and Organization **30**, 301–325.
197. Semmler, W. and A. Greiner (1996) Inventive Investment and the Diffusion of Technology. Revue Internationale de Systemique **100**(3).
198. Semmler, W. and L. Kockesen (1998) Testing the Financial Accelerator Using Nonlinear Time Series Methods. New School University, mimeo.

199. Semmler, W. and M. Sieveking (1993) Liquidity-Growth Dynamics with Corridor Stability. Journal of Economic Behavior and Organization, no. 2: 189–208.
200. Semmler, W. and M. Sieveking (1996) Computing Creditworthiness and Critical Debt. Dept of Mathematics, University of Frankfurt, mimeo.
201. Semmler, W. and M. Sieveking (1998) Credit Risk and Sustainable Debt. Paper presented at the North-American Winter Meeting of the Econometric Society, Chicago, CEM, Bielefeld University, working paper.
202. Semmler, W. and M. Sieveking (2000) Critical Debt and Debt Dynamics. Journal of Economic Dynamics and Control **24**(5–7), 1121–1144.
203. Semmler, W. and W. Zhang (2002) Asset Price Bubbles and Monetary Policy Rules: A Dynamic Model and Evidence. CEM, Bielefeld University, working paper.
204. Sieveking, M. and W. Semmler (1994) On the Optimal Exploitation of Interacting Resources. Journal of Economics **59**(4), 23–49.
205. Sieveking, M. and W. Semmler (1998) The Optimal Value of Consumption. Dept. of Economics, University of Bielefeld, mimeo
206. Sieveking, M. and W. Semmler (1999) Debt Dynamics in a Stochastic Version, Bielefeld University, mimeo.
207. Sinai, A. (1992) Financial and Real Business Cycles. Eastern Economic Journal **18**(1), 53.
208. Sharpe (1964) Capital Asset Prices. Journal of Finance **19**, 425–442.
209. Shiller, R. J. (1991) Market Volatility. Cambridge: MIT Press.
210. Shiller, R.J. (2001) Irrational Exuberance. New York: Random House.
211. Smets, F. (1997) Financial Asset Prices and Monetary Policy: Theory and Evidence. Bank for International Settlements, Working Paper no. 47.
212. Stiglitz, J. (2002) Globalization and its Discontents. New York: W.W. Norton.
213. Stock, J. and Watson (1989) New Indexes of Coincident and Leading Economic Indicators. NBER Macroeconomic Annual, ed. by O. Blanchard and S. Fischer, Chicago: University of Chicago Press.
214. Stockey, N. and R. Lucas (1995) Recursive Methods in Economics. Cambridge: Harvard University Press.
215. Summers, L. (1986) Does Stock Market Rationally Reflect Fundamental Values. Journal of Finance **41**(3), 591–602.
216. Svensson, L. (1997) Inflation Forecast Targeting. European Economic Review **41**, 1111–1146.
217. Taylor, J. (1999) Monetary Policy Rules. Chicago, University of Chicago Press.
218. Taylor, L. (2002) Structuralist Macroeconomics. New School University, book manuscript.
219. Tobin, J. (1969) General Equilibrium Approach to Monetary Theory. Journal of Money, Credit, and Banking **1**, 15–29.
220. Tobin, J. (1980) Asset Accumulation and Economic Activity. Oxford: Basic Blackwell.
221. Tobin, J. and Buiter, W. (1980) Fiscal and Monetary Policies, Capital Formation, and Economic Activity. In: von Furstenberg, G. (ed.) Government and Capital Formation, Ballinger Cambridge, MA, pp. 73–151.
222. Tong, H. (1990) Oxford Statistical Science Series, vol. 6, Non-linear Time Series. A Dynamical System Approach. Oxford: Clarendon Press Oxford.
223. Townsend, R. (1979) Optimal Contracts and Competive Markets with Costly State Verfification. Journal of Economic Theory **21**, 265–293.
224. Turnovsky, S.J. (1995) Methods of Macroeconomic Dynamics. Cambridge: MIT Press.
225. Ullah, A. and D.E.A. Giles (1998) Handbook of Applied Economic Statistics. Marcel Dekker, Inc., New York, Basel, Hong Kong.
226. Uzawa, H. (1968) The Penrose Effect and Optimum Growth. Review of Economic Studies **36**, 227–239.

227. Wilcox, D.W. (1989) Sustainability of Government Deficits Implication for Present-Value Borrowing Constraints. Journal of Money, Credit and Banking **21**, 291–306.
228. Wöhrmann, P. and W. Semmler (2002) A Toolkit for Estimating Dynamic Models in Economic and Finance. CEM, Bielefeld University, working paper.
229. Wöhrmann, P., W. Semmler and M. Lettau (2001) Nonparametric Estimation of Time-Varying Characteristics of Intertemporal Asset Pricing Models. CEM, Bielefeld University, working paper.
230. Zeldes, S. (1990) Consumption and Liquidity Constraints. Journal of Political Economy, pp. 275–298.

Index